the STORY OF GOD

for kids

for ages 6 and up

SATURATE | PUBLISHING

Every Church. Every Person. Every Place.

Story of God for Kids

ISBN:
paperback: 978-0-9968493-4-0
eBook: 978-0-9968493-5-7

Cover Design | Nathan Parry

Interior Design | Charlie Apel

Editing | Caitlin Wilson

Saturate
227 Bellevue Way NE, #224
Bellevue, WA 98004

www.saturatetheworld.com

First Edition | Printed in South Korea

Table of Contents

Introduction

THE BIBLE WAS ORIGINALLY AN ORAL DOCUMENT AND STILL IS A STORY.

The contents of the Bible were originally retold and passed along from person to person, generation to generation. After thousands of years and many generations, God in His sovereignty chose to write His story down in narrative, poetic, and apocalyptic forms, using different men guided by His Spirit.

TWO-THIRDS OF THE BIBLE IS NARRATIVE + WISDOM BOOKS = THREE-QUARTERS OF THE BIBLE IS STORY (ONE-QUARTER OF THE BIBLE IS EPISTLES).

The Biblical texts were recorded with the intent that they would be read aloud and relearned in community. In Jewish schools at the time of Jesus, the scriptures were not allowed to be read unless it was in the context of a group. Early Christians learned the stories by hearing them and retelling them together. Stories were the key for learning and experiencing God for early believers.

Bibles were not printed or available to common man in the West until the 1500s and much later in most of the world and still not available to approximately 9,000 peoples/tribes around the world. They have no written Word!

JESUS WAS A GREAT STORYTELLER!

The disciples came up and asked, "Why do you tell stories?" Jesus replied, "You've been given insight into God's kingdom. You know how it works. Not everybody has this gift, this insight; it hasn't been given

5

to them. Whenever someone has a ready heart for this, the insights and understanding flow freely. But if there is no readiness, any trace of receptivity soon disappears. That's why I tell stories: to create readiness, to nudge the people toward receptive insight." —Matthew 13:10–13 (The Message)

The Bible tells us that "Jesus spoke all these things to the crowd in parables; he did not say anything to them without using a parable." —Matthew 13:34 (NIV)

And beginning with Moses and all the Prophets, He explained to them what was said in all the Scriptures concerning Himself. ... They asked each other, "Were not our hearts burning within us while he talked with us on the road and opened the Scriptures to us?" —Luke 24:27–32 (NIV)

Do you think that Jesus was pulling a cart of scrolls down the Emmaus road with Him?! Of course not. Jesus never owned a copy of the Old Testament. There were very few copies, and they were kept exclusively in the synagogues. He told them the Story starting in the beginning.

RETHINK OUR APPROACH

We typically tell our kids what to do and how to behave and use the stories of the Bible to teach good morals. For example, when brothers are fighting, we might tell them the story of Cain and Abel with the moral being: Don't fight with your brother. However, the Bible is not a story about how to behave. It's a story about God's saving power to us.

What would it look like if we gave our children the story of God's grace, power, and love to them instead of a collection of fables to make them behave?

What if we became storytellers to teach them the way of God?

This resource is designed to help parents, leaders, and communities become storytellers and interact with children about the story. As you do this, you're learning to make disciples.

Goals of Telling the Story with Our Kids

TO UNDERSTAND, EXPERIENCE, AND INTERSECT WITH GOD'S STORY.

- To become a "story-formed" family whose lives are daily shaped by the truths of the Story.

- To make disciples of Jesus who make disciples.

- To see and experience God's "Redemptive Arc" throughout history as found in the Bible—seeing the connection between all of the stories—and seeing the Bible as one big story.

- To be moved by the Story that points to a God who constantly pursues us and desires to know us.

- To see the intersection of our stories with God's Story.

- To understand our identity differently in light of God's Story, who He is, and who He created us to be.

- To encourage us to worship God in deeper ways.

- To "live in the gospel," seeing the world differently, seeking to further God's Kingdom—to live missionally.

- To become excited about the Biblical narratives, reading and learning more about them in the Bible.

- To learn to retell these stories and help others see how they can find themselves in God's Story.

- To build Biblical community and shared experience.

.

How to Use
The Story of God

A Typical Story Session

1. REVIEW PREVIOUS NARRATIVE

Unless it's your first session, work together as a group to retell the last story you discussed together. Try not to move ahead until everyone is up to speed. This will help clear up any misconceptions or forgotten parts. This can be fun with kids and might require a few hints and nudges in the right direction.

2. TELL THE NEW NARRATIVE

This should only take around two to five minutes. Stick to the Story (more tips on this skill to come). Encourage the children to close their eyes and imagine the scene and what's happening, or you can ask them to draw the scene as they hear it.

3. RETELL THE NEW NARRATIVE

Retell the story as a group, asking everyone to participate in the retelling. Say, "Let's see if we can retell the events of this story in the order they happened." You'll need to help out a little (or a lot) at first, but throughout time the children will get better at this part. Then see if one child can retell the entire story. Again, everyone can (gently) remind him or her if he or she misses something. This retelling builds clarity and helps with retention.

4. DIALOGUE ABOUT THE NARRATIVE(S)

This is where everything really starts to open up and become alive. This part is critical in drawing out key ideas and truths from the Story. Use questions to keep discussion going, always directing the kids back to the narrative for answers and insights.

This is not the time for you to preach! You are here to guide the kids to discover truth and insight from the Story, NOT from YOU! There are several suggested questions provided as a starting point for you to use with each narrative. Do not turn this into a Q&A session! Remember, you want to facilitate genuine dialogue around the Story.

5. INTERSECT WITH THE STORY

Spend a little time with a few life-application questions, helping them connect their lives to the Story. This will naturally flow out of each dialogue time with just a little prompting through the questions provided.

Tips for Storytelling
& Dialoguing with Children

Telling the Story

GET TO KNOW THE NARRATIVE

Read the narrative over and over. Really get to know the story, what the characters are like, what they're feeling, what they sound like. Work hard to be as accurate as possible in your retelling. Children will be captivated by the story, your voice inflections, and your facial expressions.

STICK TO THE NARRATIVE

Don't mix other stuff from your knowledge of future stories into the narratives. This will only confuse the kids. They will get it.

TELL THE NARRATIVE FROM BEGINNING TO END

If you stop to answer questions, preach, or add extra parts you will only confuse people. They could also end up thinking your "helpful additions" are actually part of (and found in) the Bible! Tell the story first, and then dialogue with them. You will be interrupted. Don't worry about it. Pick up the story where you left off.

USE YOUR VOICE TO CREATE THE ATMOSPHERE

Pacing incorporates both the volume and rate at which you tell the story. Dialogue slows a story's pace down, while narrating action usually speeds it up. Repetition is a common part of storytelling—don't fear it. Use it carefully to reinforce important parts of the story. Be especially careful on how you voice God and Jesus! What is God feeling in a particular situation? Is He angry or broken-hearted and disappointed? How you voice God and Jesus will leave a huge impression on the listener as to the character and heart of God! Be appropriately animated and enthusiastic. If you read off the page with no emotion you are not really storytelling; you're just reading.

RELAX AND BE YOURSELF
Have fun with this process—it really is amazing! Be patient, take a breath, and try not to perform a story.

PRACTICE MAKES A **BIG** DIFFERENCE
Practice the story and have others listen to you and give you feedback. Like anything, you will get better the more you tell stories and lead dialogue.

READ THROUGH THE ENTIRE STORY **BEFORE** YOU BEGIN
If you are new to the Story or this method of teaching, it is imperative that you not only practice the stories, but you should read completely through all of the narratives and dialogue in your story set before beginning. This will help you connect key insights and parts of the Story found in the early narratives with parts found later on. This will make a HUGE difference in how effective your story experience will be for the participants. Understanding exactly where the Story and dialogue questions are going will make you much more successful.

Leading the Dialogue

DIRECT THE CHILDREN BACK TO THE STORY FOR ANSWERS, INSIGHT, AND TRUTH

We want to connect children to the Bible and the narratives there for the answers to their questions. Everything can be answered from within the narrative we just heard or the Story so far. Regularly ask: "Where did we see that in the story?" "Where have we seen something like this before in the story so far?" This will teach them both a biblical and systematic theology at the same time, while reinforcing the scriptures as our source of truth—not you or "group-think."

REDIRECT QUESTIONS BACK TO THE CHILDREN

Don't feel like you need to be the Bible answer man or woman. Let the group know that God gives insights into the Story that help us learn as a community. Try to affirm that every child's input is valuable.

ONLY DISCUSS INFORMATION THAT HAS EMERGED FROM NARRATIVES THAT HAVE ALREADY BEEN TOLD

Remember: "Always backward—never forward." As the adult, you might have to remind people of the stories they heard before. Repeat the stories as necessary. This is good work.

DON'T TURN THE DIALOGUE INTO "QUESTION & ANSWER" TIME

Children want to give the right answers. Allow them to wonder and use their imaginations in the dialogue. If it begins to feel like a test, ask questions that point to their lives: "How would you feel if this happened to you?" This will help them enter the story.

LEADING A DIALOGUE REQUIRES US TO ...

Let go ... of the role of expert teacher and embrace the role of co-learner, encourager, and guide.

Listen ... in expectation that God is revealing Himself to and through each person present. Pay close attention to the children's answers and the patterns that emerge in how they respond to the Story. This will reveal a lot about where their heart is.

Trust ... that God will work through the process, valuing the experience as much as the knowledge and content. Have faith that God will speak and help bring to light the truth and implications He wants to reveal.

Be patient ... allowing time to process, leaving room for different thoughts, questions, and wondering.

This is a process that involves a lot of shepherding, encouragement, and practice.

After a few stories kids will get into the rhythm of this process, and they will begin to listen and think deeply about the Story and how their own story intersects and mirrors what they are experiencing

Tell the Story

(Don't just read it—know it and bring it to life!)

I'd like to tell you a story. This story is about a being called God, who has always existed. This story, found in the Bible, describes God as the creator of all things: the heavens and the earth and everything that is alive.

God is also described as the only one who always does what is good and right and perfect—the Bible uses the word "holy" to describe Him.

Do you know what God created first?

In the Bible, God asked a man named Job, "Where were you when I laid the earth's foundation? Who decided its size and shape? Who measured it? What was it set up on, or who laid its cornerstone while the morning stars sang together and all the angels shouted for joy?"

The story begins like this. . . .

When God set the foundations of the earth, the angels were already there watching—the angels were created before everything else. When the angels saw God's power and His ability to make many different things, they sang together and shouted for joy, giving glory to God!

There was one angel who was the most beautiful of all the angels. This angel was named Lucifer, which means "bright morning star."

When Lucifer saw the other angels singing songs to God and shouting great things about God, he became jealous. He wanted them to do that for him instead of for God. He said in his heart, "I will ascend to heaven and set my throne above God's stars, and I will be like God."

Then Lucifer went and convinced a third of the angels to follow him. Although Lucifer had seen God's power in creation, he continued to lead the fallen angels, who are also called demons, in a rebellion against God.

All rebellion against God and His ways is called sin, but God knew what Lucifer was thinking and doing because He knows everything.

Because of God's perfect goodness, evil is never allowed to remain in His presence. God showed His disapproval of Lucifer and his followers by casting them down to the earth. Lucifer's name also changed; instead of being known as the bright morning star, he was now known as Satan, which means "adversary" (one who is against someone else)—and Satan is against God.

This is the story we call "Beginnings."

Retell the Story

This may seem redundant, but it is very effective in helping your kids remember and own the story. You will want to help them retell the story by giving them leading questions, such as:

- So, where did the story begin?
- What did God create first? How do we know that?
- What happened next?
- How did the angels respond to God's creation? Did they all respond the same way?
- How did Lucifer respond?

Dialogue

Remember this is a dialogue, not a quiz. The questions are a good start to draw out observations about the story, and the "answers" are just there to help you guide kids toward some key ideas.

1. **What did God create in this story?**

    -   God created everything—the earth and the angels are mentioned specifically.

2. **What were the angels' relationships with God like?**

    -   The angels were amazed by God and got to be with Him as He created.

3. **Who are Lucifer and the demons, and where did they come from?**

    -   They are angels created by God.

4. **Who is stronger: God or the angels and demons? Why?**

    -   God is stronger because He made the angels.

5. **How did Lucifer challenge God?**

    -   He said he would be like God.
    -   He deceived a third of the angels to follow him.

6. **God cast Lucifer and the fallen angels out of heaven. Why do you think He did this?**

    -   God will never allow evil to remain in His presence.
    -   God punishes evil.

7. What do we learn about God in this story?

When your kids answer, ask them, "Where in the story did you see this?"

- God is powerful.

- God is an amazing creator—He made everything with His creativity!

- God is perfect, good, and right—He is holy.

- God is amazing and deserves to be worshipped. God knows all things. He knew what was in Lucifer's heart and which angels were following him.

Application
Optional questions that may help apply the story

- **What do you like best about the story and why?**

- **What questions do you have about the story?**

- **Have you ever wanted to be in charge of something and weren't? What did you do?**

- **How are we like Lucifer/Satan?**

- **How can we be more like the angels?**

Scripture Memory Verse

O LORD, our Lord, how majestic is your name in all the earth! You have set your glory above the heavens.
PSALM 8:1

First Humans

Story from Genesis 1–23 and Psalm 8

Tell the Story

Don't just read it—know it and bring it to life!

Then God ~~decided He would~~ create another being, one who was lower than the angels, called a human. God prepared the earth to be a place for humans to live. His Spirit moved over the surface of the earth, and whenever God wanted something to be made, He simply said it and it was made.

- He made light. Do you know what He called it? He called the light day.
- What do you think He called darkness? He called the darkness night.
- Then He made the sky.
- He moved the waters back so land appeared.
- What do you think He called the waters? He called the waters seas.
- He grew plants, flowers, and trees with seeds to reproduce themselves.
- He created the sun, the moon, and the stars so there would be days and different seasons.
- He filled the seas with fish, the sky with birds, and the earth with all kinds of wild animals!

All of this creating was very important to God. He was very happy with it. In fact, after He created all these things, He looked at them and said, "This is good!"

After He had prepared the earth, God said, "Let us make humans in our image, to be like us. They will be in charge of the earth and the plants and the animals that live on it." So God formed man from the dust of the ground. Then He breathed His own breath into him, and he became alive. This man would be called Adam.

God placed Adam in a beautiful garden, a place where Adam had everything he needed to live the best kind of life. God planted all kinds of trees in the garden that produced delicious fruit so humans would always have lots to eat. God gave Adam the responsibility to take care of this garden and all His creatures. God even brought all of the animals to Adam so he could give them names!

In the middle of the garden were two special trees: the Tree of Life and the Tree of the Knowledge of Good and Evil. God told Adam he could eat fruit from any tree in the garden except for one; God warned him, "If you eat fruit from the Tree of the Knowledge of Good and Evil, you will die for sure."

Then God said, "It is not good for man to be alone. I will make a helper for him." So God caused Adam to fall into a deep sleep. While Adam was asleep, God took a rib out of Adam and made the rib into a woman. Adam later called this woman Eve, which means "Giver of Life." When this woman was made Adam said, "She is part of me." Ever since then, when people get married, they become like one person. At that time, Adam and Eve were naked, but they felt no shame.

So God created both the man and the woman in His own image. God also gave Adam and Eve the ability to continue His creation by having children. God spent time with the humans, walking with them in the cool of the day. He showed them how to live in the best possible way: a life lived close to God and under His protection—a life that is full and complete.

As God looked over all of His creation He ~~thought~~ SAID, "This is very good!" After creating all of this, God rested on the seventh day, and He made it a special day for rest.

Retell the Story

This may seem redundant, but it is very effective in helping your kids remember and own the story. You will want to help them retell the story by giving them leading questions, such as:

- So, where did the story begin?
- What did God create?
- What did He put in the middle of the garden?

Dialogue

Remember this is a dialogue, not a quiz. The questions are a good start to draw out observations about the story, and the "answers" are just there to help you guide kids toward some key ideas.

1. What do we learn about God in this story?

- God is powerful and the creator of all things.
- God showed the humans how to live in the best possible way.
- God trusts humans with the care of His creation.
- God provides and takes care of humans.
- God enjoys His creation; He said it was good in every way.
- God sets aside time for rest.

2. **How did God make humans different than the fish, birds, and animals?**
   - They are created in God's image. He breathed His own breath into them.
   - He made man from the dust and woman from man's rib.
   - He put them in charge of the earth and the animals.
   - God gives humans the ability to continue His creation by having children.

3. **What kind of relationship did God have with humans?**
   - He spent time with Adam and Eve.
   - He showed them the best possible way to live.
   - He cared about them very much.

4. **What kind of relationship did Adam and Eve have with each other?**
   - They really knew each other and loved each other.
   - They were very close.

5. **Why do you think God gave them the two trees? What did God want them to do?**
   - They could choose to obey God or not.
   - God wanted them to choose to obey, to choose life (the Tree of Life).

6. **Why did God rest?**
   - He was finished with His work; He didn't need to create anymore.
   - He was very happy with what He made—it was very good.

Application

Optional questions that may help apply the story

- **What do you like best about the story, and why?** (amaze)

- **What do you think God wants us to do?** (apply)

Scripture Memory Verses

And God blessed the seventh day and made it holy, because on it he rested from all the work of creating that he had done.
GENESIS 2:3

When I consider your heavens, the work of your fingers, the moon and the stars, which you have set in place, what is man that you are mindful of him, the son of man that you care for him? You made him a little lower than the heavenly beings and crowned him with glory and honor. You made him ruler over the works of your hands; you put everything under his feet.
PSALM 8:3-6

Tell the Story

Don't just read it—know it and bring it to life!

One day, Satan went to Eve disguised as a snake. He asked Eve, "Did God really say you can't eat any of the fruit in the garden?" Eve told him, "No, we can eat from any tree in the garden. It's only the Tree of the Knowledge of Good and Evil we are not allowed to eat from—or even touch—or we will die."

Trying to trick Eve, the snake said, "You won't really die! God knows that when you eat the fruit from that tree your eyes will be opened, and you will become just like Him! You will know everything, both good and evil." When Eve saw how delicious the fruit looked, she thought, "We will know everything!" Then she took some of it and ate it. She also gave some to Adam, who was with her, and he also ate it. They chose not to believe God and to believe the lie.

As soon as they ate the fruit, they realized they were naked; they were naked before, but now they were ashamed of their nakedness. They picked fig leaves and put them together around their hips to cover their nakedness.

Toward evening, they heard God walking in the garden, so they hid themselves in some trees. God called to them, "Where are you?" and Adam answered, "I heard you coming and was afraid because I was naked, so I hid."

God answered, "Why are you ashamed of being naked? Did you eat the fruit I told you not to eat?" Adam said, "It was the woman you gave me. She gave me some." Then God said to Eve, "How could you do this?" Eve replied, "The snake tricked me into eating the fruit." So God said to the snake, "Because you have done this, you and your kind are cursed to crawl on your belly and eat dust the rest of your life. You will be the enemy of men, women, and their sons. You will bite his heel, but he will crush your head." (Punishment & Promise)

~~God's heart was broken because they disobeyed Him~~. They didn't GOD believe God loved them and wanted what was best for them. He had to do something about it. Remember, God always does what is right and true, and He also cannot let disobedience just go. So God punished Adam and Eve by throwing them out of the Garden, outside of His care and protection.

Because Adam and Eve did not follow God's ways, they were now going to get sick, feel pain, and eventually die. God told them, "Now because of what you have done, your life will not be easy. You will have many problems and feel pain, then you go back to the ground where you came from."

God still loved Adam and Eve. He even created clothing for them out of animal skins so they would be covered outside of the garden. After removing Adam and Eve from the garden, God stationed powerful angels outside of the entrance to the garden. A flaming sword flashed back and forth, guarding the way to the Tree of Life. Humans would no longer be able to eat from the Tree of Life and live forever.

Retell the Story

This may seem redundant, but it is very effective in helping your kids remember and own the story. You will want to help them retell the story by giving them leading questions, such as:

- So, where did the story begin?
- What did the snake say to Eve?
- What did Adam and Eve do after they ate the fruit?

Dialogue

Remember this is a dialogue, not a quiz. The questions are a good start to draw out observations about the story, and the "answers" are just there to help you guide kids toward some key ideas.

1. What do we know about this snake? What did he try to do? How?

- He was bad—evil.
- He tried to make them not believe what God had said.
- He lied about what God had said by telling Eve the fruit would make her like God.
- Where have we seen this before?

2. Why was it a bad idea for them to eat from the Tree of Knowledge of Good and Evil?

- God told them not to.
- They would get punished for it; they would have pain and die.
- They wanted to be God and to be able to determine what is right of wrong instead of God.

3. **What happened to their relationship with God and each other because of their disobedience?**

   - They were now afraid of God and embarrassed with each other.

   - They were kicked out of the garden where they would live close to God.

4. **Why do you think God punishes them for their disobedience?**

   - Because God is perfect and good and holy, He will never allow evil to remain in His presence.

   - His holiness requires that sin be punished.

5. **What do we learn about people in this story?**

   - People can be deceived into believing wrong things.

   - People can choose God's ways or their own.

   - When people sin, they tend to hide and blame.

6. **What do we learn about God in this story?**

   - God knows all things. He knew Adam and Eve had eaten from the tree.

   - God punishes sin—the snake's head would be crushed by man; the man and woman would experience pain and death.

   - God keeps His promises; He said they would die if they ate of the fruit of the Tree of the Knowledge of Good and Evil, and eventually they would.

   - God is gracious. He still took care of them. He made clothing for them out of animal skins.

Application

Optional questions that may help apply the story

- **What do you like best about the story, and why?**

- **How are we like Adam and Eve?**

Scripture Memory Verse

For the wages of sin is death, but the gift of God is eternal life in Christ Jesus our Lord.

ROMANS 6:23

CAIN & ABEL

Story from Genesis 4

4

When we last heard about Adam and Eve, what had happened?

- Because Adam and Eve did not follow God's ways, they were now going to get sick, feel pain, and die eventually.

- God removed Adam and Eve from the garden and put powerful angels outside of the entrance to the garden. A flaming sword flashed back and forth, guarding the way to the Tree of Life.

- Humans could not eat from the Tree of Life and live forever.

Tell the Story
Don't just read it—know it and bring it to life!

What do you think will happen next now that Adam and Eve are outside the garden?

I'm going to tell you a story about their two sons …

After leaving the garden, Adam and Eve had two sons named Cain and Abel. When they grew up, Cain became a farmer, and Abel became a shepherd, looking after sheep.

At harvest time, Cain brought to God a gift from what his farm produced, while Abel brought several of the very best lambs from his flock.

God accepted Abel and his offering of the lambs, but He did not accept Cain and his offering.

This made Cain very angry and upset. "Why are you so angry?" God asked Cain. "Why do you look so discouraged? You'll be accepted if you do what's right. But if you refuse to do what's right, then watch out! Sin is crouching like a lion at your door, waiting to attack and destroy you, and you must bring it under control."

Later, Cain suggested to his brother, Abel, "Let's go out into the fields. . . ." While they were there, Cain attacked and killed his brother. This was the first murder described in the Bible.

Afterward, God asked Cain, "Where is your brother, Abel?"

"I don't know!" Cain replied. "Am I supposed to keep track of him wherever he goes?"

But God said, "What have you done? Listen . . . your brother's blood cries out to me from the ground! You have to leave this place and the ground you have dirtied by making your brother bleed here. Now it will not produce great crops for you, no matter how hard you work! From now on you will be homeless, on the run, constantly wandering from place to place."

Cain replied to God, "My punishment is more than I can handle! You have removed me from my land and from your presence; you have made me a wanderer, on the run. All who see me will try to kill me!"

God replied, "No! They will not kill you. Anyone who tries to hurt you will receive seven times your punishment."

God put a mark on Cain to warn anyone who might try to kill him that they would be in trouble if they hurt him. Then Cain left God's presence and traveled to the land east of the garden.

Retell the Story

This may seem redundant, but it is very effective in helping your kids remember and own the story. You will want to help them retell the story by giving them leading questions, such as:

- Where did the story begin?
- What happened next?
- Whose offering did God accept?
- Who got mad and killed his brother?
- What did God to say to him then?
- Who had to leave God's presence?

Dialogue

Remember this is a dialogue, not a quiz. The questions are a good start to draw out observations about the story, and the "answers" are just there to help you guide kids toward some key ideas.

1. Why did Cain kill his brother?

- He was upset that God accepted his brother's offering and not his.

2. Why did Cain have to leave?

- He had dirtied the ground with his brother's blood—he had killed his brother.
- God will never allow evil to stay around Him.

3. Did Cain's sin destroy him like God said it would?

- Yes, he had to go away from God and lost the chance to be in God's presence.

4. **How is Cain like his parents, Adam and Eve?**

   - He decided to do things his way instead of trust God.

   - He ended life—his brother's. His parents ended their chance at eternal life with God.

5. **How did God show his love for Cain in the story?**

   - He told Cain to get his sin under control and gave him a warning.

   - He gave Cain a mark so no one would kill him, even though he had killed his brother. He told Cain that anyone who tried to hurt him would receive seven times his punishment.

6. **What do we learn about God in this story?** *(When your kids answer, ask them, "Where in the story did you see this?")*

   - God is powerful.

   - God knows all things. Nothing we do is hidden from Him.

   - God is perfect, good, and right—He is holy.

   - God gives us chances, but He cannot be around sin.

   - God is loving—He protected Cain from being hurt.

Application

Optional questions that may help apply the story

- **What do you like best about the story, and why?**

- **What questions do you have about the story?**

- **Have you ever been really upset with your brother/sister/ friend? What did you do about it?**

- **How are we like Cain?**

- **How can we bring ourselves "under control" when we are feeling really angry?**

Scripture Memory Verse

If you do what is right, will you not be accepted? But if you do not do what is right, sin is crouching at your door; it desires to have you, but you must master it.

GENESIS 4:7

The Flood

5

Review the last stories a bit, focusing more on the most recent story, Cain and Abel.

- **What do we know about Creation?**

- **What is the story of Adam and Eve?**

- **What happened with Cain and Abel?**

Tell the Story

Don't just read it—know it and bring it to life!

The number of humans on the earth grew rapidly. Not only did sin spread from Adam and Eve to their sons, but it spread to their son's children and their children's children and on and on. Even though humans were created in God's image, everyone chose to disobey God. They constantly hurt each other with their words, their actions, and their bodies. God saw that people's thoughts were completely evil— all of the time. This ~~broke His heart and~~ displeased God & made Him wish He had never created humans.

God decided to start over. He said, "I will completely wipe out this human race I created. I am sorry I ever made them."

But there was one man, named Noah, who had a close relationship with God. Noah was the only man living on earth at that time who had this kind of relationship with God. God said to Noah, "I have decided to cover the earth with a flood, destroying everything alive! However, I will give you a plan to keep you safe."

37

God then told Noah to build a large boat called an ark, giving him specific instructions about how big to make it and what this boat should be like. God said to him, "Make a boat from wood and seal it with tar, inside and out. Then build many decks and stalls for animals inside of it. I promise to keep you safe in this ark! Bring seven pairs of animals I have approved for sacrifices and one pair of each of the others. These animals will come to you to be kept alive. Remember: Take enough food for your family and for all the animals."

Noah did everything exactly as God told him to do. Just as God said, the floods came; water burst out from the earth, and rain poured from the sky. When the waters came, Noah, his family, and all the animals came on board the ark. As the waters rose, the boat floated safely on the surface. The flood covered even the tallest mountains, and all living creatures on the earth were destroyed, except for those on the ark.

After forty days the rains stopped. Many months passed as the waters slowly began to dry up. For weeks, Noah sent out a dove to see if it could find dry land. Finally the dove returned with an olive leaf in its mouth. So Noah sent the dove out again, and when it didn't come back, he knew it was safe to return to land.

As soon as Noah came off of the ark, he built an altar, chose pure animals from every species, and sacrificed them to God as a symbol of thankfulness and worship. God was pleased with Noah's sacrifice and said, "I will never again curse the earth, destroying all living things with a flood, even though people's thoughts and actions are bent toward evil from childhood. As a symbol of my promise I will hang a rainbow in the clouds. When you see a rainbow, this will remind you of my promise to you."

Then God told Noah and his sons, "I have put all animals under your control. You can use them for food, but you must never eat animals that still have their lifeblood in them. Those who murder must be punished by death. Life is in the blood, and all life belongs to me!"

God blessed Noah and his sons, telling them to have many children and once again fill the earth with people.

Retell the Story

This may seem redundant, but it is very effective in helping your kids remember and own the story. You will want to help them retell the story by giving them leading questions, such as:

- Where did the story begin?
- What happened next?
- Who was Noah?
- What did God tell him to do? Did he obey?

Dialogue

Remember this is a dialogue, not a quiz. The questions are a good start to draw out observations about the story, and the "answers" are just there to help you guide kids toward some key ideas.

1. Why did God flood the earth and destroy everything? Do you think that was a good idea?

- The heart of every human was completely evil.

2. What do the stories we have heard so far show us about what humans are like?

- Since the fall of Adam and Eve, every person has disobeyed God.

- Humans care more about taking care of things themselves than letting God take care of things for them.
- Humans don't trust God.

3. From this story, how does God feel about humans?

- He was heartbroken they did not choose His way AGAIN.
- Compassionate: He saved the human race and made a promise not to destroy us again.

4. What was God saying to Noah (and all humans) by creating a rainbow?

- God wants to give us the best possible life; He always provides a way for us.
- He always takes care of us.
- He gives us hope.

5. What did God say to Noah about the blood from the sacrifices? Why was this important?

- All life belongs to God, and life is in the blood. It is God Himself who gives life.

6. What does the story teach us about God?

- God is powerful. He controls the rain and the animals.
- God will never allow evil to remain in His presence.
- The flood shows us that God is serious about wiping out sin.
- God is the source of all grace. He saved Noah and his family.
- God warned Noah and his family about what would happen, just like with Cain.
- He promised never to destroy the earth again, even though He knew man would continue to sin. He is merciful and gives us chances.
- God knows all things. He knew what was in the heart of every man.

Application

Optional questions that may help apply the story

- What do you like best about the story, and why?

- What questions do you have about the story?

- When is it hard to believe that God is taking care of you?

- How does God give you hope when you are in a rough situation?

Scripture Memory Verse

Whenever the rainbow appears in the clouds, I will see it and remember the everlasting covenant between God and all living creatures of every kind on the earth.

GENESIS 9:16

Covenant

Review the last stories a bit, focusing more on the most recent story, "The Flood."

- What is the story of Adam and Eve?

- What happened with Cain and Abel?

- What did we learn about God and people in the story of "The Flood"?

Clarify some words you'll read in the story.

- What are descendants?

- What are generations?

- What is an inheritance?

Tell the Story

Don't just read it—know it and bring it to life!

I'm going to tell you a story that starts many years after Noah and his family made a new start …

Noah's descendants forgot about God and how He had spared them in the flood. They made plans to construct a great city out of brick. They said, "Let's build a monument to ourselves that reaches to the heavens to show how great we are."

God saw how people were gathering together to honor themselves instead of Him. At that time everyone on earth spoke the same language, so God gave people different languages to make it harder for them to join together in rebellion. Then He scattered them all over the earth.

A few generations later, God established a special relationship and a promise with a man named Abram. This special promise was called a covenant, representing the deepest of all agreements between two people.

God made this covenant with Abram …

- … I will make you the father of a great nation—famous throughout history.
- … I will bless you and make your name great, and you will be a blessing.
- … I will bless those who bless you and curse those who curse you.
- … The entire earth will be blessed through your descendants.

This was an amazing promise God was making. He was choosing to bless the entire earth through one family of people! There was just one problem: Abram's wife, Sarai, had not been able to have children, so how would the earth be blessed through their descendants? Not to mention they were getting old. At that time Abram was about seventy-five and Sarai about sixty-five!

God told Abram, "I want you to leave your country and your family and go to the land I will show to you." So Abram and his family left, as God had said, and went to a land called Canaan. There God told Abram, "Look as far as you can see in every direction. I am giving this land to you and your descendants." This land of Canaan would now be called the "Promised Land."

Some time passed, and Abram and Sarai still did not have a child. Abram asked God, "What good are all of your blessings if I don't even have a son? I am getting old, and soon I will have to give my inheritance to one of my servants."

God replied to Abram, "No, you will have a son who will inherit everything I have promised you." Then God took Abram out beneath the night sky and said, "Look up into the heavens and count the stars if you can. Your family will be like this—too many to count!" Abram believed what God said, so God called him "righteous" because of his faith.

More years passed, and Sarai became impatient with not having a child. She asked her servant, an Egyptian woman named Hagar, to have a child for her. Abram agreed with this plan. Hagar became pregnant and gave birth to a boy named Ishmael. However, Hagar and Sarai were not getting along. During Hagar's pregnancy, she began to hate Sarai. In return, Sarai treated Hagar terribly.

When Abram was ninety-nine, God appeared to him again, saying, "I am the mighty God; serve me with your entire life and live purely. I will keep my covenant with you for many generations to come. I am changing your name to Abraham, which means 'father of many nations.' Remember this: I will always be your God, and you will always be my people." Then God added, "I am also changing your wife's name to Sarah, which means 'mother of many nations.' Very soon she will be blessed with a son. You are to name this son Isaac."

Both Abraham and Sarah laughed to themselves in disbelief of God's promise. Abraham wondered, "How can I become a father at one-hundred years old? How can Sarah have a baby when she is almost ninety?"

Sarah thought, "How could a worn-out woman like me have a baby? My husband is even older than I am!"

Abraham asked God, "Would you pass on your blessing through my son Ishmael?"

But God said, "No. Sarah will have a son about a year from now, and it is through him I will pass on my blessing. Why would you laugh at this thought, Abraham? Is anything too hard for me?"

Sure enough, a year later—exactly as God had said—Sarah gave birth to their first son, naming him Isaac, which means "laughter." Isaac's birth caused Sarah and Hagar to hate each other again, so Hagar and Ishmael were sent away and not allowed to live with Abraham's family.

The birth of Isaac was the beginning of God completing the promise He made to Abraham. God desired for Abraham's descendants, called the Hebrews, to be a new kind of people who would show the world what it means to live in God's ways.

Retell the Story

This may seem redundant, but it is very effective in helping your kids remember and own the story. You will want to help them retell the story by giving them leading questions, such as:

- What happened next?
- Why did God give us many languages?
- Did Abraham and Sarah believe God at first? Why not?

Dialogue

Remember this is a dialogue, not a quiz. The questions are a good start to draw out observations about the story, and the "answers" are just there to help you guide kids toward some key ideas.

1. **Why did God stop the people from building a monument to themselves?**

2. **What do we learn about Abraham from the story? About Sarah?**
   - God chose him to carry out His blessing.
   - He was old!

- He trusted God and left his home.
- Even though they trusted God in the end, they found it hard to believe what God had said.

3. Where in the story was it hard for Abraham to believe the promise?

- Abraham thought he would have to give up his inheritance to one of his servants.
- Abraham and Sarah laughed at God's promise and thought, "How could this happen?"

4. What was God's relationship with Abraham?

5. What do we call this special promise God made with Abraham? How is it special?

6. Where have we seen God make a promise or covenant before?

- With Cain and with Noah.

7. What did God promise to Abraham?

- To make him the father of a great nation, giving him many descendants.
- To bless and protect him.
- To bless all the nations of the earth through him.

8. What does this promise tell us about what God is like?

- God wants to bless all people.
- God has chosen a family (nation) to be His blessing and to live in His ways.
- God will protect and bless His people.

9. If you had to wait twenty-five years for a promise of God to come true, would you still believe God?

Application

Optional questions that may help apply the story

- **What questions do you have about the story? What from this story will you remember the most?**

- **How does this story make a difference in your life?**

- **What is the most important promise you've ever made? Did you keep it?**

- **What do you think it means to be blessed by God?**

- **How do people in our world build "monuments" to themselves?**

Scripture Memory Verse

Is anything too hard for the LORD?
GENESIS 18:14

Isaac

Story from Genesis 22

Review the last stories a bit, focusing more on the most recent story, "Covenant."

- What happened with Cain and Abel?
- What did we learn about God and people in the story of "The Flood"?
- What did Abraham and Sarah learn about God?

Before beginning, remind them what "descendants" means.

Tell the Story

Don't just read it—know it and bring it to life!

You won't believe what happened next. . . .

Some time later God tested Abraham. He called out to him, "Abraham!"

"Yes, I am listening," he replied.

God said, "I want you to take your son Isaac, whom you love, up to the top of the mountain and offer him as a sacrifice."

The next morning Abraham awoke early, saddled up his donkey, and chopped some wood for the offering. After everything was ready, Abraham and his son Isaac took two of their servants and set out for the mountain. About three days into their journey, they saw the mountain in the distance. Abraham told his servants, "Stay here. Isaac and I are going up the mountain to worship, then we will come right back."

Abraham took the knife and the fire from the servants, and he placed the wood for the sacrifice on Isaac's shoulders. As they were walking up the mountain, Isaac became curious and asked, "Father, we have the wood and the fire, but where is the lamb we are going to sacrifice?" Abraham told him, "God Himself will provide a lamb."

When they arrived at the top of the mountain, they built an altar and placed the wood on it. Then Abraham tied Isaac up and laid him on the altar over the wood. Then he took the knife and lifted it to kill his son as a sacrifice to God. At that moment the Angel of God shouted to him from heaven, "Abraham! Abraham!"

"Yes, I'm listening," he replied.

The Angel said, "Put down the knife. Do not hurt your son. It's clear you trust me because you did not hesitate to give me what you love the most." Then Abraham looked behind him and saw a ram with his horns caught in a bush. He caught the ram and offered it to God in place of his son. Abraham named that place at the top of the mountain "God Will Provide."

Then the Angel of God spoke to Abraham again, telling him, "God wants to tell you: Because you have not refused to give me your son, I will bless you greatly! Your family will multiply into millions—like the stars in the sky and the sand on the beaches! Your descendants will defeat their enemies. The entire earth will be blessed through your family because you chose to obey me."

Then Abraham and Isaac went down the mountain, met up with their servants, and returned home.

Retell the Story

This may seem redundant, but it is very effective in helping your kids remember and own the story. You will want to help them retell the story by giving them leading questions, such as:

- So, where did the story begin?

- What happened next?

- What did Abraham do? What didn't Abraham do?

- What did the Angel tell Abraham at the end?

Dialogue

Remember this is a dialogue, not a quiz. The questions are a good start to draw out observations about the story, and the "answers" are just there to help you guide kids toward some key ideas.

1. **How did Abraham feel about his son Isaac?**

   - Abraham loved his son.

2. **How did God and Abraham get along?**

   - Abraham had a special relationship with God—chosen as the blessing.

   - Abraham had faith God would keep His promise.

   - Abraham listened to God (and His angel).

3. **What did Abraham say to his servants?**

4. **What does this story show us about Abraham?**

5. **What does this story show us about Isaac?**

   - Isaac trusted his father.

6. **What was Abraham risking to obey God in this story?**

    - The promise of God blessing the entire earth through his descendants.

7. **Where have we seen sacrifice before in the stories? Why did people do this? What is God teaching through these sacrifices?**

    - God providing clothing from animal skins for Adam and Eve.
    - Cain and Abel, Noah's sacrifice to show thankfulness to God and show Him as the provider.
    - Noah: After the flood God made it clear that life is in the blood.
    - Isaac: God provided an animal in place of Isaac—life for life.

8. **Would you obey God if He asked you to do this?**

9. **What does this story teach us about God?**

    - He provides for His people.
    - He tests people's faith.
    - He desires to bless us.
    - He keeps His promises.

Application

Optional questions that may help apply the story

- **What questions do you have about the story?**

- **What from this story will you remember the most?**

- **How does this story make a difference in your life?**

- **What is the greatest gift you've ever given someone? ... ever received?**

- **What is something one of your family members has done for you that really made a difference in you life?**

Scripture Memory Verse

God Himself will provide.
from GENESIS 22:8

Jacob & Esau

Story from Genesis 25

Review the last stories a bit, focusing more on the most recent story, "Isaac."

- What did we learn about God and people in the story of "The Flood"?

- What did Abraham and Sarah learn about God?

- How did God show up in the Abraham and Isaac story?

Briefly discuss what "inheritance" and "deceiver" mean to make sure all children understand.

Tell the Story

Don't just read it—know it and bring it to life!

When Isaac was forty years old, he married Rebekah. Isaac prayed hard for his wife because she could not have a child. God answered his prayer, and Rebekah became pregnant with twins. The two children fought with each other inside her womb.

She prayed and asked God, "Why is this happening to me?"

God told her, "Your sons will become two rival nations. One nation will be stronger than the other, and the older son will serve the younger son."

When the first son was born he was very red and hairy; he looked like he was already wearing clothing! They called him Esau, which sounds like the word for "hair." Then the other twin was born with his hand grabbing Esau's heel. They named him Jacob, which means "grabbing the heel" but can also mean "deceiver."

As the boys grew up, Esau became an expert hunter who loved the outdoors. His brother Jacob liked to stay indoors and live quietly in the tents. Isaac loved Esau and all the wild game he would bring home, but Rebekah favored Jacob.

Once when Jacob was cooking some stew, Esau came home exhausted from hunting and said to Jacob, "I'm starving! Give me some of that stew you've made."

Jacob replied, "All right, but trade me your inheritance for it."

"Hey—I'm dying of starvation!" said Esau. "What good is my inheritance to me if I starve?"

Jacob demanded, "Swear to me right now that you will give me your inheritance." So Esau gave an oath, much like a promise, trading away his inheritance and his rights as the firstborn son. Then Jacob gave Esau some bread and stew. Esau quickly ate and drank and went on his way—not thinking about the fact he had just given up his inheritance.

Years later, when Isaac was old and almost blind, he called for Esau and said, "I am an old man now, and I will die soon. Hunt some wild game for me and prepare it just the way I like it. Then before I die I will pass on the blessing that belongs to you, my firstborn son."

Rebekah overheard this conversation. When Esau left to go hunting, she said to Jacob, "Do exactly as I tell you. Go and bring back two of the finest goats from our flocks, and I'll prepare your father's favorite dish from them. Take the food to your father; then he will eat it and give you the blessing instead of Esau."

Jacob replied, "Mother, he won't be fooled that easily. Esau is hairy, and my skin is smooth! What if he touches me? He'll see I'm trying to trick him, and then he'll curse me instead of blessing me."

"Just do as I say!" Rebekah demanded.

Jacob brought back two of their best goats, and Rebekah made Isaac's favorite meal. Then she put Esau's best clothes on Jacob and made him a pair of long hairy gloves from the skin of the goats. Then Jacob took the meal to his father, pretending he was Esau.

"The voice is Jacob's, but the hands are Esau's," Isaac said to himself.

"Are you really my son Esau?" Isaac asked.

"Yes, of course!" Jacob answered.

"If you are, come here and kiss your father," Isaac said. So Jacob went and kissed Isaac. When he did this Isaac smelled his clothes and was finally convinced he was really Esau. Isaac gave his blessing to Jacob, saying, "May God pass on to you the blessing he promised to Abraham. Your family will grow large and become a great nation, and other nations will become your servants. God will bless those who bless you and curse those who curse you."

As soon as Isaac had blessed Jacob, Esau returned from his hunting trip. When he learned Isaac had given his blessing to his brother, he wept out loud, "Father, bless me, too!"

But Isaac said, "Your brother was here and tricked me. He has carried away your blessing."

Esau hated Jacob and said to himself, "After my father is dead, I will kill Jacob."

Rebekah found out Jacob was in danger and sent him far away to live with his uncle. On his journey God appeared to Jacob, saying, "I am the God of your grandfather and father. I am giving you and your descendants this land. Your family will grow large and be a blessing to the entire earth! I will be with you and protect you wherever you go, giving you everything I have promised."

God blessed Jacob with great wealth and twelve sons! Jacob's name was changed to Israel, which means "struggler with God." The Hebrews would later be called the people of Israel, named after Jacob.

Many years later Esau forgave his brother, Jacob. Then Jacob and his growing family moved back to the Promised Land of Canaan.

Retell the Story

This may seem redundant, but it is very effective in helping your kids remember and own the story. You will want to help them retell the story by giving them leading questions, such as:

- So, where did the story begin?
- What happened next?
- How did Jacob get Esau to give him his birthright?
- How did Rebekah and Jacob trick Isaac?

Dialogue

Remember this is a dialogue, not a quiz. The questions are a good start to draw out observations about the story, and the "answers" are just there to help you guide kids toward some key ideas.

1. **From this story, what do we learn about Jacob? Esau? Rebekah?**

2. **What did God tell Rebekah about the children in her womb? How might that have affected her actions?**

3. **Why do you think Esau gave up his inheritance easily?**

4. **Why do you think Jacob wanted his father's blessing?**

5. **Why would God pass on His blessing to Jacob when he tricked his father to get it?**

6. **What blessing is God passing on through Abraham, Isaac, and now Jacob?**

7. **In what ways are we also like Jacob? How does this give us hope?**
   - We are all sinners just like Jacob.
   - None of us do anything to deserve God's blessings, but still He blesses us.

8. **What does the story teach us about God?**
   - God is powerful. He was able again to cause Rebekah, a barren woman, to conceive (just as He had done with Sarah).
   - God knows all things. He knew the future of the boys while they were still in the womb.
   - He knew the older would serve the younger.
   - God is the source of all grace. God blesses us even when we don't deserve it.
   - Jacob was a continual deceiver, but God set up His covenant with him and loved him.
   - God keeps His promises. He passed the covenant He made with Abraham on to his son Isaac and on to Jacob. Each time He promised to bless all the nations of the earth through them.
   - God is patient with our selfishness.

Application

Optional questions that may help apply the story

- **What questions do you have about the story?**

- **What will you remember most about this story?**

- **How does this story make a difference in your life?**

- **Where in your life has God blessed you?**

- **Why do you think God uses people to bless others?**

- **Have you ever been unkind to a person and then been blessed anyway?**

Scripture Memory Verse

I am with you and will watch over you wherever you go.
GENESIS 28:15

Joseph

Story from Genesis 37–39, 41–50

9

Review the last stories a bit, focusing more on the most recent story, "Jacob and Esau."

- What patterns do you notice about God in these stories?

- What did Abraham and Sarah learn about God?

- How did God show up in the Abraham and Isaac story?

- What did God tell Jacob in the last story?

There is a section in this story where Potiphar's wife tries to seduce Joseph and then accuses him of raping him. You decide whether that is a section of the story you wish to tell and discuss, depending on the age of the children in your group. You may want to just say, "Potiphar's wife lied about Joseph to get him in trouble, and Potiphar had him thrown into the king's prison."

Tell the Story

Don't just read it—know it and bring it to life!

Israel (Jacob) and his twelve sons now lived in the Promised Land. Out of all of his sons, Israel loved Joseph the most and made him a beautiful coat with long sleeves. When Joseph was seventeen, he helped his brothers tend the cattle and reported to his father anything they did wrong.

Joseph's brothers grew to hate him because he was their father's favorite. They hated him even more when he told them he had dreams about the future where he saw all of them bowing down to him!

One day Joseph went to check on his brothers, and they grabbed him, ripped off his beautiful coat, and threw him into a deep hole. The brothers decided to sell Joseph to slave traders who were passing by on their way to Egypt.

They tore up their brother's coat, soaked it in goat's blood, and brought it to their father, saying, "We found this in the field. It's Joseph's, isn't it?"

Israel examined it and said, "Yes, this is my son's coat. A wild animal must have attacked and eaten him." He began to weep, saying, "I will mourn my son's death until the day I die!"

Meanwhile, the slave traders sold Joseph to a man named Potiphar, the head guard for Pharaoh, the king of Egypt. Potiphar noticed God was with Joseph and blessed everything he did. He promoted him, putting him in charge of his entire household and business.

Now Joseph was a young, handsome man, and Potiphar's wife began to desire him. She constantly pressured him to sleep with her. But Joseph refused, saying, "That would be a terrible thing and a great sin against God!"

One night after Potiphar got home, his wife lied and told him, "The Hebrew slave you brought here tried to rape me." Potiphar became furious and threw Joseph into the king's prison. However, God gave him favor with the head of the jail. God was with Joseph, continuing to give him success in everything he did.

Before long Joseph was put in charge of the other prisoners and everything that happened there! God also gave Joseph the ability to explain the prisoners' dreams to them.

A few years later Pharaoh had some dreams that troubled him. In one of them he saw seven fat cows being eaten by seven thin cows! None of Pharaoh's wisest men could explain to him what this meant. One of the servants who had been in prison with Joseph told Pharaoh about his ability to interpret dreams.

Pharaoh had Joseph brought to him and asked, "Can you really interpret dreams?"

Joseph replied, "That is beyond me, but God will tell you what your dreams mean and ease your worry."

Pharaoh shared his dreams, and Joseph interpreted them, saying, "For the next seven years Egypt will have more than enough food. This will be followed by seven years of a terrible famine that will spread over the land, when there will not be enough food for everyone."

The king was so impressed with Joseph that he put him in charge of everything in Egypt—second in power only to Pharaoh himself! During the next seven years Joseph traveled throughout Egypt, making sure plenty of food was being stored up in each city. Joseph was only thirty years old at the time.

Seven years passed, and the famine came, spreading throughout the world. People from all over the land came to Egypt to buy food from Joseph.

When Israel realized his family was running out of food, he sent his sons to Egypt. When the brothers arrived to buy food, they didn't recognize Joseph and bowed down before him.

At first Joseph was harsh with his brothers, even accusing them of being spies and putting them in prison. Later, after many meetings and two journeys by his brothers, Joseph finally revealed who he was, saying, "I am Joseph, your brother whom you sold as a slave!"

The brothers stood there speechless, shocked, and afraid! They would never have thought Joseph could still be alive.

But Joseph spoke to them kindly and said, "Don't be afraid. God turned your evil into something good. He put me in this high position so I could save the lives of many people. Now I will take care of you and your families."

When Pharaoh heard that Joseph's brothers had come, he invited Israel and his entire family to live in Egypt. He gave them a plot of his best land, plenty of food, and new clothing!

The family of Israel came to live in Egypt, escaping the drought and enjoying the blessings God had given to Joseph.

Retell the Story

This may seem redundant, but it is very effective in helping your kids remember and own the story. You will want to help them retell the story by giving them leading questions, such as:

- Where did the story begin?
- What did Joseph's brothers do to him when he was younger?
- How did Joseph treat his brothers later?
- What did Joseph say to his brothers at the end?

Dialogue

Remember this is a dialogue, not a quiz. The questions are a good start to draw out observations about the story, and the "answers" are just there to help you guide kids toward some key ideas.

1. From this story, what do we learn about Joseph's brothers?

2. Why didn't Joseph's brothers like him?

3. **What do we learn about Joseph from the story?**

   - He was a dreamer.
   - He told on his brothers.
   - He was blessed by God and successful in all he did.
   - He trusted God in a bad situation.
   - He made good decisions in temptation.
   - He wanted to take care of his family.

4. **How did Joseph respond in the difficult situations he faced? What do you think about how he responded—did it help?**

5. **How does God continue His promise to the Hebrews in the story?**

   - He did not let the descendants of Abraham—Israel and his family—die in the famine.

6. **What does the story teach us about God?**

   - God knows all things. He can work things out for His plan.
   - He shows them what will happen in the future.
   - He promoted Joseph and blessed him in order to save many people.
   - God keeps His promises. The things revealed in the dreams came true just as God said they would.
   - God is powerful. He can control the elements by bringing a famine.
   - God chooses to work through people who are not perfect.

7. **Where have we seen God take a situation that seemed bad and turn it into good (either from the stories or from your own life)?**

Application

Optional questions that may help apply the story

- **What questions do you have about the story?**

- **What will you remember most about this story?**

- **How does this story make a difference in your life?**

- **How does Joseph's life inspire you?**

- **Do you like things in life planned out or as a surprise?**

Scripture Memory Verse

The LORD was with Joseph and gave him success in whatever he did.

GENESIS 39:23

10

Moses

Story from Exodus 1–4

Review the last stories a bit, focusing more on the most recent story, "Joseph."

- What patterns do you notice about God in these stories?

- How did God show up in the Abraham and Isaac story?

- What did God tell Jacob?

- How has God continued to keep His promises in the story of Joseph?

Vocabulary to discuss (especially for young children) before, in between tellings, or after the story: famine, slavery, and clumsy.

Tell the Story

Don't just read it—know it and bring it to life!

The family of Israel had moved to Egypt and was enjoying the blessings God had given Joseph. Years passed, and Israel's family multiplied so quickly they began to fill Egypt! Soon a new king ruled Egypt who didn't remember how Joseph had saved them from the great famine. This king, called Pharaoh, told his people, "The Israelites are becoming a threat to us. There are too many of them! If we don't stop them now, they could join our enemies and fight against us."

The Egyptians made the Israelites their slaves and treated them horribly. Pharaoh even gave an order to have every newborn son of the Israelites killed by drowning them in the Nile River.

One Hebrew family put their baby son in a basket and floated him down the Nile in hopes of saving his life. Pharaoh's daughter discovered this baby crying in the basket and felt sorry for him. Moses' sister, who followed the basket from a distance, offered to help Pharaoh's daughter find a mother to nurse the baby.

Pharaoh's daughter agreed, but she didn't know she was hiring Moses' own mother to take care of him! The princess took the baby home to raise him in the king's palace and named him Moses (which means "to draw out") because she drew him out of the water.

Many years later, after Moses had grown up, he went out to where his own people were and watched them being forced to work as slaves. He witnessed an Egyptian beating one of the Hebrews. Moses looked around to see if anyone was watching, killed the Egyptian, and buried him in the sand.

When Pharaoh heard about this he tried to have Moses killed, but Moses escaped to the wilderness and started a new life as a shepherd.

Several years later a new Pharaoh came into power and continued to punish the Israelites in slavery. The people of Israel cried out to God for help and deliverance. God heard their cries and felt deep concern for them. He did not forget the covenant promise He made to Abraham, Isaac, and Jacob.

One day while Moses was tending sheep he noticed a bush that was on fire, but it wasn't burning up. He said to himself, "That's amazing! I've got to go over and see this."

God called out to him from the bush, "Moses, Moses!"

"Yes, here I am!" Moses answered.

"Don't come any closer," God told him. "Take off your sandals because you are standing on holy ground. I am the God of your father, the God of Abraham, the God of Isaac, and the God of Jacob." Moses hid his face in his hands because he was afraid to look at God.

Then God told him, "I have heard my people's cries for deliverance, and I have come down to rescue them. I have chosen you to meet with Pharaoh and lead my people out of Egypt."

Moses begged God to send someone else, saying, "Who am I? I'm not a good speaker. I'm clumsy with my words."

God said, "Who created mouths? Who gives people the ability to speak, hear, and see? I will help you speak clearly, and I will tell you what to say. Be prepared, though—Pharaoh is stubborn and will not listen." God also told Moses he could bring his brother Aaron with him to help him speak to Pharaoh.

Then Moses asked, "Who should I tell them has sent me?"

God replied, "I AM WHO I AM. Tell them that I AM has sent you—the God of Abraham, Isaac, and Jacob. This is my name for every generation."

Then Moses and Aaron went to Pharaoh and said, "This is what the God of Israel says: 'Let my people go!'"

You won't believe what happened next. …

Retell the Story

This may seem redundant, but it is very effective in helping your kids remember and own the story. You will want to help them retell the story by giving them leading questions, such as:

- Where did the story begin?
- Where did Moses grow up?
- What did he do when he saw one of his own people being treated badly?
- Where did God talk to Moses for the first time?

Dialogue

Remember this is a dialogue, not a quiz. The questions are a good start to draw out observations about the story, and the "answers" are just there to help you guide kids toward some key ideas.

1. **How did the Israelites get into Egypt? How were they treated when they first arrived? How did that change?**

2. **Why did Moses remove his sandals when he talked to God?**

3. **Why do you think Moses was afraid to look at God?**

4. **What did God call Himself in the story? What do you think this means?**
   - I will always be—before you and after you.
   - God cannot be contained in a name—too amazing for words.

5. **What do we learn about Moses from this story?**
   - Moses was a sinner and a murderer, but God still chose to use him.
   - He felt weak, but God used him anyway.

- He obeyed God and went with his brother Aaron to talk to Pharaoh.

6. **How does Moses get along with God? How do the people of Israel get along with God?**

7. **What does this story teach us about God?**
   - He is powerful.
   - He keeps His promises.
   - He cares for people.
   - He is able to deliver and protect all who cry out to Him.
   - He wants to use people to represent Him.
   - He allows suffering.
   - His ways are sometimes hard for us to understand at first.
   - He gives us everything we need to do His work, even if we don't think we are "good enough" or "ready" sometimes.

Application
Optional questions that may help apply the story

- **What questions do you have about the story?**

- **What will you remember most about this story?**

- **How does this story make a difference in your life?**

- **Has God ever used you when you were afraid or unsure of yourself? How? What did you learn?**

- **How has God taken care of your family in the past?**

Scripture Memory Verse

I am the God of your father, the God of Abraham, the God of Isaac and the God of Jacob.

EXODUS 3:6

The Passover

Story from Exodus 5–15

Review the last stories a bit, focusing more on the most recent story, "Moses."

- What patterns do you notice about God in these stories?

- What did God tell Jacob in the story?

- How has God continued to keep His promises through the story of Joseph?

- What did God call Himself in the story of Moses, and what does that tell us about Him?

Tell the Story
Don't just read it—know it and bring it to life!

Our last story told us a little about Moses and his life. Now he goes on to talk with Pharaoh, Egypt's leader. You'll never guess what happens next. …

Moses and his brother Aaron met with Pharaoh and pleaded with him, "Let the Israelites leave Egypt for just three days to worship God. If you choose not to do this, God will punish the Egyptians severely."

Pharaoh was stubborn and would not listen. He said, "Who is this God that I should listen to Him? I don't know your God, and I am not letting you leave. You are just trying to create a distraction. Now, get back to work!"

After their meeting with Pharaoh things got worse for the Israelites. Pharaoh forced them to work faster and longer hours. Cruel slave masters pushed them to work harder and harder as they made bricks from mud and straw and worked in the fields.

God sent a series of horrible plagues on the Egyptians and their land, but these plagues did not have any effect on the Israelites. The first plague turned the Nile River into blood. All of the fish died, and the water smelled terrible and was undrinkable.

The second plague brought a mob of frogs that covered the entire country. These frogs were everywhere—in their bedrooms, their kitchens, and even their pots and pans!

The third and fourth plagues brought gnats and flies. They covered all of the people and animals. Pharaoh's magicians tried to copy each of these plagues but couldn't create gnats. They cried to Pharaoh, "God must be doing this to us!"

After each of these plagues Moses returned to Pharaoh and asked him to let the Israelites go so they could worship God. But Pharaoh was stubborn and would not listen.

The fifth plague brought severe disease to Egypt's livestock, but none of the Israelites' cattle became sick!

The sixth plague caused the Egyptians to break out with horrible sores all over their bodies—so bad they couldn't sit or lay down!

As each of the plagues hit, Pharaoh would say, "Enough! If you stop the plagues, I will let you leave." But after God stopped the plagues, Pharaoh still would not let them go. God had made Pharaoh even more stubborn, and he refused to listen.

The seventh and eighth plagues brought hail and locusts that destroyed every tree and plant in the land. The locusts swept down and ate everything that wasn't wiped out by the hail.

The ninth plague brought complete darkness over the land for three days. No one could see anything except for the Israelites, who still had light in their homes.

Despite all of these horrific events, Pharaoh still would not let the Israelites leave! God told Moses, "Pharaoh's stubbornness will give me the opportunity to do even greater miracles in Egypt."

So God would send one final plague. . . .

Moses warned Pharaoh about this final plague, saying, "This is what God says: 'About midnight I will pass through Egypt. Every firstborn son will die—rich or poor—from Pharaoh's son on down. The Egyptians will weep loudly, but the Israelites will not be touched. Then you will beg the people of Israel to leave.'"

Moses left his meeting with Pharaoh burning with anger. In spite of this warning, Pharaoh still refused to let them go.

Then Moses and Aaron gave the Israelites instructions from God on how they could be saved from this plague. They told the people, "Each family is to select a sacrifice: a year-old male lamb or goat that is pure and without any defects (problems). Be careful not to break any of its bones. Then take the blood from this sacrifice and put it on the door frames of your home. This will be a sign from God to pass over your home and spare your firstborn."

So the people of Israel did exactly what God told them to do. At midnight God came through Egypt and took the life of every firstborn son, but He passed over the homes that had blood on their door frames.

All of Egypt woke during the night because of the loud weeping. Someone had died in nearly every Egyptian home, including Pharaoh's own son. The Egyptians begged the Israelites to leave right away.

That night the Israelites, now numbering more than two million, set out to return to their Promised Land of Canaan. God guided them through the wilderness with a pillar made of clouds during the day and a pillar of fire at night.

Meanwhile Pharaoh changed his mind again and sent his armies after the Israelites to catch them. As Pharaoh and his army approached, the people of Israel saw them in the distance and began to panic because the Red Sea was in front of them. They turned against Moses, complaining, "Our slavery back in Egypt was better than dying out here in the wilderness!"

Moses told the people, "Don't be afraid. God will rescue you today. He will fight for you!"

Then God told Moses to stretch out his hand over the sea. As he did this, God brought a huge wind that opened up a dry path for them to walk across! Pharaoh and his armies began to follow behind the Israelites. God told Moses to stretch out his hand again. This brought another huge wind that blew the sea back over Pharaoh and his armies, completely destroying them!

The people of Israel were in awe of God's amazing power. They put their trust in God and also in His servant Moses. They sang songs, danced, and celebrated how God had saved them!

Retell the Story

This may seem redundant, but it is very effective in helping your kids remember and own the story. You will want to help them retell the story by giving them leading questions, such as:

- Where did the story begin?
- What were some of the problems God's people, the Israelites, had?
- How did they finally get out of Egypt?

Dialogue

Remember this is a dialogue, not a quiz. The questions are a good start to draw out observations about the story, and the "answers" are just there to help you guide kids toward some key ideas.

1. **Why is this story called the "Passover"?**

2. **Can you remember God's promise to Abraham? What parts of God's promise to Abraham do we see beginning to be fulfilled?**

3. **How many descendants did Abraham have in just a couple of generations?**

4. **How did God treat the Israelites' enemies?**

5. **Why do you think God would harden Pharaoh's heart? What did Pharaoh's stubbornness allow God to do?**

6. **Where is water mentioned in this story? How is this significant?**

7. **Where have we seen water mentioned in previous stories?**

8. **What did God specifically say about the animal they were to sacrifice? Why did it need to be pure?**

9. **Why do you think God required blood to be put on the Israelites' door posts to be saved? What does blood represent, and what does it mean?**

10. **How might you have felt that Passover night as a Hebrew? Would you have doubted God would save you in this situation?**

11. **What does this story teach us about God?**

   - He keeps His promises (covenant, warnings to Pharaoh).

   - He is able to deliver and protect all who cry out to Him.

   - He is powerful.

   - He cares for people.

   - He is the source of grace.

   - He wants to use people to represent Him.

   - He allows suffering.

   - His ways are sometimes hard for us to understand at first. (He warned Pharaoh.)

   - He punishes injustice and wrong.

Application
Optional questions that may help apply the story

- **What questions do you have about the story?**

- **What will you remember most about this story?**

- **How does this story make a difference in your life?**

- **What questions do you have from the story?**

- **When is a time in your life you refused to listen to someone's good advice?**

- **Have you ever celebrated a Seder Dinner or Passover Celebration? What was it like?**

Scripture Memory Verse

I will take you as my own people, and I will be your God. Then you will know that I am the LORD your God, who brought you out from under the yoke of the Egyptians.

EXODUS 6:7

Review the last stories a bit, focusing more on the most recent story, "Passover."

- What patterns do you notice about God in these stories?

- How has God continued to keep His promises through the story of Joseph?

- What did God call Himself in the story of Moses, and what does that tell us about Him?

- What does Passover mean?

Tell the Story

Don't just read it—know it and bring it to life!

It wasn't long after the Israelites left Egypt that they began complaining again to Moses. They complained about not having enough to eat and not having water to drink. They kept nagging at him, "Why did you make us leave Egypt? We had plenty to eat and drink there. Did you lead us into the wilderness to die?"

Moses cried out to God, "What am I going to do with these people? They're about to kill me!"

Each time the Israelites ran out of food or water, God provided for them through a miracle; He sent birds to their camp for them to eat, covered the ground with a flaky bread-like food, and even made water pour out of a rock for them to drink!

Two months after leaving Egypt, the Israelites set up camp at the bottom of Mount Sinai. Moses climbed up the mountain so he could meet with God.

There God spoke to him, saying, "Tell my people this, 'You saw how I carried you on eagles' wings and rescued you from Egypt. Now if you obey me and keep my covenant, you will be my treasured people—a kingdom of priests—set apart to represent me."

When Moses came down the mountain he told the people what God said. They all agreed, "We will do everything that God asks us to do. Really, everything."

Then God told Moses, "Gather the Israelites at the bottom of the mountain so I can speak to them." As the people gathered, God warned them, "Do not climb the mountain or even touch the edge or you will be put to death."

Right then, a powerful storm rolled in, and a dark cloud covered the mountain. God spoke to them from a blazing fire on top of the mountain, giving these commands: "I am your God who rescued you from slavery in Egypt. Put me above everything else. Do not worship other things. Do not misuse or disrespect my name. Remember to set aside a day each week to rest and worship me. Honor your parents. Don't murder or steal or lie. Do not sleep with anyone but your husband or wife; be faithful. Don't lust after what others have; be satisfied with what I give you."

As God spoke, the people trembled with fear and moved away from the mountain! Moses told them, "Don't be afraid. God is showing you His awesome power. From now on let your fear of Him keep you from sinning!"

As the people stood in the distance, Moses climbed back up into the dark clouds where God was. On the mountain God gave Moses more instructions, called laws, to give to Israel. These laws gave specific details about things, such as how to treat neighbors and enemies, how to handle conflicts, what is fair punishment, when to work and rest, when to celebrate and worship, and what offerings are acceptable to God.

Another time Moses went up on the mountain for forty days and forty nights with his helper, Joshua. God gave Moses two stone tablets. On these tablets were the details of the covenant written by God's finger!

While Moses was away on the mountain, the people went to his brother Aaron and said, "We don't know what happened to Moses. Make us a god we can see who will lead us!"

Aaron created an idol in the shape of a golden calf and put it on an altar for them to worship. He told them, "Here is the god that saved you from Egypt!" The next day the people had a wild party as they worshipped the gold calf.

When God saw how the Israelites were acting, He said to Moses, "I have seen enough of these people's stubbornness and rebellion. I am going to destroy all of them with fire and create a new nation from your children."

Moses begged God not to kill them, and God withdrew His threat, allowing them to live.

When Moses returned to camp and saw the people worshipping the calf, he was so angry that he smashed the stone tablets on the ground! Then he took the calf, ground it up into powder, mixed it with water, and made the people drink it! The next day Moses returned to the mountain to ask God to forgive his people.

God responded, "Whoever has sinned against me must be punished." God sent a plague to punish those who had worshipped the calf. About 3,000 of the Israelites died from this plague.

(Pause)

Soon after that God also said to Moses, "I am full of mercy and grace. I am slow to get angry and full of love and faithfulness. I show my love by forgiving rebellion and sin, but I will not let sin go unpunished. This is the covenant I will make with the people of Israel: I will show my awesome power through you and remove those who oppose you, but you must always listen to me and obey my commands."

Moses met with God for another forty days and forty nights. God wrote on a new set of tablets the details of how to live in the covenant. Moses gave these tablets to the people of Israel so they could follow them and live in His ways and enjoy His blessings.

Retell the Story

This may seem redundant, but it is very effective in helping your kids remember and own the story. You will want to help them retell the story by giving them leading questions, such as:

- Where did the story begin?
- What were some of the instructions and laws God told Moses to share with the people?
- Why was Moses upset with the people when he came down off the mountain?

Dialogue

Remember this is a dialogue, not a quiz. The questions are a good start to draw out observations about the story, and the "answers" are just there to help you guide kids toward some key ideas.

1. **What is a covenant?**

   - A promise

2. **What was the covenant God was talking about? Whom was it given to first?**

3. **Do you think the Israelites could keep their side of the covenant? How?**

4. **Would God remove His covenant if they did not obey Him?**

   - Partially—He may not bless them and protect them, but ultimately He chooses to save them to show how great He is, not always basing this on how sinless they are.

5. **What is the purpose of the commandments and laws? Why do you think God is specific about these things?**

6. **Which of these commandments do you think is the hardest to keep?**

   - You may want to ask some specific questions about each of the commandments.

7. **What do God's commandments and laws show us about Him?**

8. **What happens when we follow in God's ways? Where have you seen this in the stories?**

   - God's people must live a certain way to reflect the character of the holy God.

Application

Optional questions that may help apply the story

9. **What questions do you have about the story?**

10. **What will you remember most about this story?**

11. **How does this story make a difference in your life?**

12. **How do you figure out the right way to live? What happens when we are left to figure this out for ourselves?**

13. **What rules do you have a hard time following? Why?**

14. **When are rules good or helpful?**

Scripture Memory Verses

Love the LORD your God with all your heart and with all your soul and with all your strength.
DEUTERONOMY 6:5

For the LORD your God is a merciful God; he will not abandon or destroy you or forget the covenant with your forefathers, which he confirmed to them by oath.
DEUTERONOMY 4:31

Sacrifices

13

Story from Exodus 25-40, Leviticus 1-5, 12-23,
Numbers 3, 9-14, and 27-33

Review the last stories a bit, focusing more on the most recent story, "Law and Commands."

- What patterns do you notice about God in these stories?

- What did God call Himself in the story of Moses, and what does that tell us about Him?

- What sacrifices happened during Passover?

- How did God share the instructions for His covenant with Moses and the people of Israel?

You may want to define "sacrifice" for your group, depending on the age of the children. Talk about it as a verb (to sacrifice) and as a noun (a sacrifice). You may also want to draw a simple diagram of the Tabernacle. Making a big one and having children step into the different places or making a smaller one and placing little figures in it would help make it realistic for them.

Tell the Story
Don't just read it—know it and bring it to life!

God had just given the people of Israel specific instructions about how to live in His ways and remain close to Him in a covenant relationship. During one of Moses' trips up the mountain, God also gave Moses specific instructions about how to build a holy tent called the Tabernacle. God said, "Build a special place for me to live among the people I love."

Moses gathered the very best craftsmen and workers, and they began building the Tabernacle in the center of their camp.

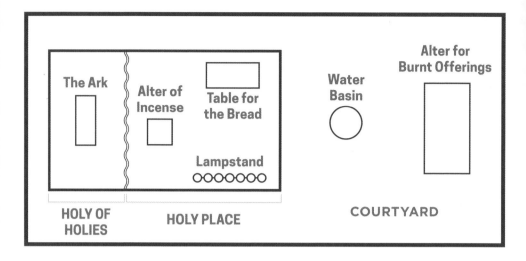

The tent was divided into two rooms. The large outer room was called the Holy Place. Inside of this room was a stand that held seven oil lamps called a Menorah. These lamps burned day and night and symbolized God's constant protection and watch over His people. Next to this was a table with twelve loaves of bread on it, reminding them God would always provide for their needs. Also in the Holy Place was a gold altar where incense burned. Incense reminded them of God's nearness and was also a symbol of their prayers rising to God.

The second inner room was called the Holy of Holies. A thick curtain hung from the ceiling of the tent all the way down to the floor, separating it from the Holy Place. This room contained a special wooden chest called the Ark of the Covenant. Inside the Ark were the stone tablets God wrote on and gave to Moses. On top of the Ark was a gold cover called the Mercy Seat where the presence of God would come.

When the Israelites finished building the Tabernacle, God showed His presence was there by covering the top of it with a cloud during the day and a pillar of fire at night. Whenever the cloud or fire would move, they would pack up camp and follow it.

God told the people of Israel, "When you realize you have sinned, you must confess it and bring an offering to me. Then I will remove your sins and forgive you." Because of His love for the Israelites, God was providing a way for them to substitute the life of an animal that was pure and without defects in place of their own—a life for a life.

Everyday people would bring sacrifices to God in the courtyard of the Tabernacle. This system of sacrifice continued for hundreds of years, but these sacrifices were only a symbol of what was to come. God was preparing a final sacrifice that would pay for the world's sins once and for all.

Retell the story so far, and then continue. . . .

At this time the Israelites organized themselves into twelve groups—called tribes—according to which of the twelve sons of Israel (Jacob) they were a descendant.

Moses' brother Aaron was the oldest of the descendants of Levi, Israel's firstborn son. God chose Aaron and his sons to represent the people as priests. They had the special job of bringing the people's offerings to God. The priests were the only ones allowed inside the Tabernacle. If anyone else tried to come near God's presence they would die. No one was allowed to go inside the Holy of Holies except the high priest, Aaron, on a special day called the Day of Atonement.

God said to Moses, "In addition to the weekly Sabbath, you should set aside time for festivals where everyone comes together to worship, celebrate, and rest." So the Israelites held several festivals each year—some lasted for weeks!

During one of their fall festivals was this special Day of Atonement. God said, "This will be a special day where you will all be made right with me. Today you will find forgiveness and cleansing from all your sins."

Then God told the Aaron what he must do on the Day of Atonement. He said, "You must follow all of my instructions completely or you will die.

Make sure you are completely clean, without sin on the inside and out. Wear the special clothes made for this occasion." (God went on to describe the special underclothing and elaborate robe Aaron should wear.)

Then He continued, "Sacrifice a young bull as payment for your sins and the sins of your family. Then dip your finger in the blood from this bull and sprinkle it on the cover of the Ark and then seven times on the front of the Ark."

"Then find two spotless goats and sacrifice one of them as a substitute for the sins of all of the Israelites. Take its blood and sprinkle it on the cover and front of the ark as you did with the bull's blood. I will accept this and forgive all the sins and rebellion of the people. Remember, blood represents life; in this blood you will find life and atonement for your sins."

After this Aaron was to bring in the other goat that was still alive, called the scapegoat (also called the Ahzazel, which means to "take away"). God told him, "Lay both of your hands on its head and confess all of the people's sins, putting them on the head of the goat. Then lead this goat far away into the wilderness. The people's sins will be taken away with it, never to be seen again."

Aaron and the people of Israel followed God's instructions carefully. Because of this, the people were made right with God once again and given atonement for their sins. This was a holy day the people of Israel continued to celebrate year after year.

Retell the Story

This may seem redundant, but it is very effective in helping your kids remember and own the story. You will want to help them retell the story by giving them leading questions, such as:

- Where did the story begin?
- What did the Tabernacle look like?
- What was inside the rooms?
- What happened on the Day of Atonement?

Dialogue

Remember this is a dialogue, not a quiz. The questions are a good start to draw out observations about the story, and the "answers" are just there to help you guide kids toward some key ideas.

1. **What was the purpose of the Tabernacle?**

2. **Why do you think no one was allowed to go in to the Holy of Holies?**

3. **What was the purpose of the sacrifices people brought to God?**

4. **Who was the first high priest God chose? Where have we seen him before? Do you think he deserved to be high priest?**

5. **What does the word "atonement" mean?**

6. **What stands out to you as most important about the Day of Atonement?**
   - The detail and order in which things happened. This was necessary so the high priest did not die in the presence of God.

- The importance of blood to pay for sin—life for life. We have now seen this several times. Life must be substituted for another life to pay for sin.

- God is holy and separate, and no one can casually come into His presence. There is even a tradition that when the high priest went into the Holy of Holies, he tied a rope around his ankle in case he died before God. Then he could be pulled out of the Holy of Holies without someone else going in after him and dying.

7. Why were there two goats used on the Day of Atonement? Why was this important?

- The first goat was a payment for sins; the second goat allowed for the removal and taking away of those sins.

8. What does this story teach us about God?

- God is holy and will not allow sin to remain in His presence. Not just anyone could enter the Holy of Holies—only the high priest once a year, and then only if he had first paid for his sins!

- God is the source of grace. He makes a way for man to come to Him and for his sins to be paid for.

- God wants us to listen to Him and live in His ways, not our own.

- God wants us to come to Him with great respect and awe.

- God loves His people and desires to be near them.

Application
Optional questions that may help apply the story

- **What questions do you have about the story?**

- **What will you remember most about this story?**

- **How does this story make a difference in your life?**

- Have you ever thought that if you were good enough, God would let you into His presence or into heaven? Does this story challenge or reinforce that idea?

- How do you think we should come to God? How do you come to God?

- Has anyone ever received punishment you deserved? What happened?

Scripture Memory Verses

They will know that I am the LORD their God, who brought them out of Egypt so that I might dwell among them.
EXODUS 29:46

It is the blood that makes atonement for one's life.
LEVITICUS 17:11

Judges, Kings, & Prophets

14

Story from Deuteronomy, Joshua, Judges, 2 Samuel, 2 Kings
Prophecies from 2 Samuel 7, Isaiah 7, 9, 40, 53, 61,
Psalm 22, Micah 5, and Zachariah 12

Review the last stories a bit, focusing more on the most recent story, "Sacrifices."

- What patterns do you notice about God in these stories?

- What sacrifices happened during Passover?

- How did God share the instructions for his covenant with Moses and the people of Israel?

- What do you remember about "atonement"?

This is a longer story spanning a huge length of time. You may want to break it into two parts or even three, depending on the ages of the children. Drawing a large timeline and letting children stand on it or point to/draw pictures along the way may help them understand the scope of time this story represents.

Tell the Story
Don't just read it—know it and bring it to life!

The people of Israel continued on their journey back to the Promised Land. God covered the Tabernacle with a cloud during the day that changed to a pillar of fire at night. When this cloud moved they followed it and set up camp wherever it stopped.

But when the people of Israel got closer to Canaan, they would not enter the land because they were afraid of the people who lived there. God's punishment for not trusting Him was to make them wander in the dessert for forty years. This was a time filled with struggle and complaints against Moses and God.

As Moses neared the end of his life, he reminded the people of Israel of all of God's promises, laws, and commandments. Moses challenged them, "You must love God with all of your heart, mind, soul, and strength, for He is your life!"

Then Moses said to Joshua in front of all of the Israelites, "Be strong and courageous! Now you will lead these people into the land God promised us. Do not be afraid or discouraged; God will never leave you or forget about you." (If you remember from a previous story, Joshua was Moses' assistant who went up the mountain with him to meet with God.)

After Moses died, Joshua became the new leader of Israel and led them to recapture the Promised Land from their enemies. As the Israelites entered the land, God told them to drive out all the people who lived there because they were full of evil. But the Israelites didn't listen and eventually started worshipping the false gods of the people who remained in Canaan. This led into many other sins. Because of their disobedience, God removed His protection and allowed other nations to come into Canaan and overpower them.

As they were defeated, the people of Israel began to suffer, so they begged God for help and forgiveness. God once again forgave them and sent leaders, called judges, to lead them in defeating their enemies. (These are not like judges we have today but more like generals.) Battle after battle, Israel conquered their enemies at every border. In victory the people would worship God, but soon after the people would turn away from God again and live their own way.

Unfortunately this became a pattern from generation to generation. The people of Israel would come to God and worship Him when they needed help, but when things were going well, they returned to worshipping other things. This was a time where everyone did what was right in their own eyes.

Because other nations were ruled by kings, the people of Israel complained to God, saying, "We want a human king we can see to rule over us." So God appointed a king named Saul to rule Israel. However, because of Saul's disobedience, God eventually removed him as king.

Then God searched for a king who would love Him and live in His ways. He chose a young boy named David. When David grew up and was made king, God blessed him and the Israelites greatly. David deeply loved God and tried to live in his ways. God told David, "One of your descendants will rule Israel forever—His kingdom will never end!"

Solomon succeeded his father, David, and became the wisest and richest king in history. Solomon prayed to God, "Give me your wisdom so I can rule the people the right way."

God answered his prayer and gave Solomon great wisdom; in fact, rulers traveled from all over the world just to hear him. Solomon wrote books, such as Proverbs and Ecclesiastes, that are full of the wisdom God gave him.

Under Solomon's leadership the people of Israel enjoyed peace and great prosperity. The Temple was built in the capital city of Jerusalem to replace the Tabernacle. This temple was a more-permanent symbol of God's presence remaining with the people.

However, later on Solomon married foreign wives who led him into worshipping false gods. Because of Solomon's failures, God allowed civil war to break out and the Israelites divided into a northern kingdom called Israel and a southern kingdom called Judah. Eventually kings that worshipped false gods led both of these kingdoms.

Because of their rebellion, God removed His protection from both Israel and Judah and allowed other nations to come in and conquer them. The Israelites were forced out of the Promised Land, and many were taken away to be slaves once again.

During the time of these kings, God sent prophets as messengers, calling people to return to His ways and follow His commandments. These prophets warned the Israelites what would happen if they continued to rebel against God. They also told people about a coming King, one who would rule forever and save them—a Messiah.

God gave the prophets visions of what this Messiah would be like. (Listen carefully to these, as they will tie into some future stories.)

Prophets, such as Isaiah, told them that …

> … He will be a descendant of King David.
>
> … a virgin will give birth to Him in Bethlehem.
>
> … a messenger from the wilderness will challenge people to prepare for His coming.
>
> … He will bring good news and healing to the poor, brokenhearted, and sick.
>
> … He will do no wrong, living a life without sin.
>
> … He will be beaten, whipped, and wounded—all so we can have peace, healing, and forgiveness.
>
> … He will be silent when faced with accusations. He will be put on trial and thrown in prison.
>
> … His hands and feet will be pierced. He will be killed like a criminal, then buried in a rich man's tomb.
>
> … God will lay the punishment and guilt for all of our sins on Him. His life will be made an offering for us.
>
> … Because of Him, many will be made right with God.

After these prophets, God did not speak to humans again for 400 years.

Retell the Story

This may seem redundant, but it is very effective in helping your kids remember and own the story. You will want to help them retell the story by giving them leading questions, such as:

- Where did the story begin?
- Who are some of the leaders of the Israelites?
- What were some of the prophecies about the coming King?
- What does God do for the Israelites along the way?

Dialogue

Remember this is a dialogue, not a quiz. The questions are a good start to draw out observations about the story, and the "answers" are just there to help you guide kids toward some key ideas.

1. **Why did God tell the Israelites to drive out everyone who lived in Canaan? What happened?**

2. **What is the pattern the Israelites got into?**

3. **What was the role of the prophets? What did the prophets foretell about the Messiah?**

From all of the stories so far . . .

4. **What have you seen for the first time in these stories?**

5. **What common themes run through all the stories?**
   - God wants us to live closely with Him—listening and obeying.
   - He provides the best possible way of life for us to live.

- God wants to rescue His creation and bring them back to Himself. He will go to amazing lengths to accomplish this.

- Our sins require sacrifice—a life for a life.

6. **What have we learned about what humans are like? Where have we seen that?**

7. **What have we learned about what God is like? Where have we seen that?**

   - He does what is good, right, and perfect—He is holy.

   - He is powerful, is creative, knows all things, has control over the elements, punishes rebellion, keeps His promises, does not allow evil to remain with Him, provides a way of forgiveness, loves His creation, provides us with the best way to live, wants to protect us and bless us, wants us to continue His blessings, and much more!

Application

Optional questions that may help apply the story

- **What questions do you have about the story? What do you wonder about?**

- **What will you remember most about this story?**

- **How does this story make a difference in your life?**

- **Are we like the Israelites? What patterns do we get into that are not good?**

- **When you think of your future what do you put the most hope in?**

- **From all of the stories so far, which person is most like you? Why?**

- **What does it mean for you to live in God's ways right now?**

Scripture Memory Verses

Now choose life, so that you and your children may live and that you may love the LORD your God, listen to his voice, and hold fast to him. For the LORD is your life.
DEUTERONOMY 30:19-20

He is the Rock, his works are perfect, and all his ways are just. A faithful God who does no wrong, upright and just is he.
DEUTERONOMY 32:4

Be strong and courageous. Do not be terrified; do not be discouraged, for the LORD your God will be with you wherever you go.
JOSHUA 1:9

The Birth Of Jesus

15

Story from Matthew 1–2, Luke 1–2

Review the last stories a bit, focusing more on the most recent story, "Judges, Kings, and Prophets."

- What patterns do you notice about God in these stories?

- How did God share the instructions for His covenant with Moses and the people of Israel?

- What do you remember about "atonement"?

- At this point in the story, how long has it been since God has spoken to His people through the prophets?

Tell the Story

Don't just read it—know it and bring it to life!

Now 400 years had passed since God had spoken to His people. The Israelites, called Jews, had been under the control of other nations for hundreds of years. They were now ruled by the Romans, the most powerful empire that had ever existed. The Jews were still waiting and hoping for a king who would come to save them and lead them into victory.

Finally, God sent an angel to a young woman named Mary in the town of Nazareth. She was engaged to be married to a man named Joseph, who was a descendant of King David.

The angel, named Gabriel, appeared to her and said, "Don't be afraid, Mary. God has chosen to bless you! You will become pregnant and have a son, and you are to name him Jesus (which means 'God saves'). He will become a King whose Kingdom will never end!"

Mary asked the angel, "But how can I have a baby? I am still a virgin."

The angel replied, "This will happen supernaturally by God's Spirit, so this baby will be called God's Son. Remember: Nothing is impossible with God!"

Mary said, "I am God's servant. May everything you have said come true!"

After that Mary sang to God, thanking Him for choosing to bless her. Just as the angel had said, Mary became pregnant.

When Joseph found out Mary was expecting a child, he decided to break off their engagement quietly. The law would have permitted him to have her killed if she had an affair.

But one night Joseph had a dream. An angel appeared to him and said, "Joseph, do not be afraid to take Mary as your wife. The child in her is from God. You are to give Him the name Jesus, for He will save the people from their sins."

So Joseph took Mary as his wife, but he did not sleep with her until after the baby was born.

Months later, as Joseph and Mary were traveling to Bethlehem, the time came for Mary to give birth. No rooms were available for them at the local inns, so they found an animal stable—and that is where their baby was born.

They named the boy Jesus, meaning "the Lord is salvation," just as the angel had told them. Mary wrapped Him in strips of cloth and laid Him in a feed trough.

That night a group of shepherds were out in the fields taking care of their sheep when an angel suddenly appeared and frightened them.

The angel said, "Don't be afraid. I am bringing good news for everyone! The one who will save you, the Messiah, has been born tonight in Bethlehem! You will know it's Him when you find a baby in a stable wrapped in strips of cloth."

The shepherds said to each other, "Let's go to Bethlehem as fast as we can to see the miracle God told us about."

When the shepherds ran into town they found Joseph, Mary, and the baby in the stable just as the angel had said. After this they went and told everyone what they had heard and seen—and the people were truly amazed!

A few months later, wise men traveled from distant lands to find the newborn king. A star had guided them from the east to Bethlehem and stopped over the place where Mary and Joseph were living. As the wise men entered the house they were overcome with joy and kneeled down and worshipped Jesus. They brought Him expensive gifts of gold, spices, and perfumes.

Eventually Joseph and Mary moved back to Nazareth where Jesus grew strong, wise, and full of God's grace. When Jesus was twelve years old, He and His family attended the annual Passover Festival in Jerusalem. (Do you remember the first Passover?)

On the way home, Joseph and Mary assumed Jesus was in their caravan but traveling with some of their other relatives. Later, when they stopped to sleep for the night, they realized He was nowhere to be found. In a panic, Joseph and Mary went back to Jerusalem to look for Jesus.

Three days later they finally found Him. He was in the temple courts, discussing deep questions with the religious teachers. The teachers were all amazed at His understanding and insights. His parents didn't know what to think.

"Son!" His mother said to Him. "Why have you done this to us? Your father and I have been frantic and have searched for you everywhere."

"But why did you need to search?" Jesus asked. "You should have known I would be in my Father's house." Joseph and Mary didn't understand what He meant. Jesus returned to Nazareth with His parents and was obedient to them. His mother thought deeply about what had happened.

Jesus grew in both height and wisdom and was loved by God and everyone who knew Him.

Retell the Story

This may seem redundant, but it is very effective in helping your kids remember and own the story. You will want to help them retell the story by giving them leading questions, such as:

- Where did the story begin?
- What happened in this story leading up to Jesus' birth?
- What happened after it?

Dialogue

Remember this is a dialogue, not a quiz. The questions are a good start to draw out observations about the story, and the "answers" are just there to help you guide kids toward some key ideas.

1. **What did we learn about Joseph? ... about Mary?**

2. **What was unique about Jesus' birth? Where was He born?**

3. **Why do you think it was important for Jesus to be born of a virgin mother?**

4. **Who was Jesus a descendant of? How might this be important?**

   - David—He's the promised king.

   - Abraham—He's the promised one through whom all the nations would be blessed.

5. **What can we learn from the shepherds and how they responded to the angel?**

6. **What else did your hear in this story that reminds you of what the prophets said about the promised Messiah?**

   - See the end of the previous story for a list of prophecies.

7. **What does the name "Jesus" mean?**

   - The Lord is salvation.

   - Another name given to Jesus was Emmanuel, which means "God with us"!

8. **We have all probably heard this story before as part of the "Christmas story." What jumps out at you as new or different?**

Application

Optional questions that may help apply the story

- **What questions do you have about the story? What do you wonder about?**

- **What will you remember most about this story?**

- **How does this story make a difference in your life?**

- **What do you imagine people thought when they had been told the Messiah had been born?**

- **How would you have reacted? Would you have expected His entrance to the world to be different?**

- **If God sent Jesus to give the world a great gift, why do you think we focus so much on what we get at Christmas?**

- **How can we best celebrate and remember the birth of Jesus? What can YOU do to celebrate this personally?**

Scripture Memory Verses

She will give birth to a son, and you are to give him the name Jesus, because he will save his people from their sins.
MATTHEW 1:21

Do not be afraid. I bring you good news of great joy that will be for all the people. Today in the town of David a Savior has been born to you; he is Christ the Lord.
LUKE 2:10-11

Baptism & Temptation

16

Story from Matthew 3–4, Mark 1, Luke 3–4, and John 1

Review the last stories a bit, focusing more on the most recent story, "The Birth of Jesus."

- What patterns do you notice about God in these stories?

- What do you remember about "atonement"?

- How did Jesus' birth fulfill the words of the prophets?

- Up until now, what similarities do you see between Jesus and God?

SCENE 1: BAPTISM

Tell the Story
Don't just read it—know it and bring it to life!

God sent a messenger named John to tell people to get ready because the Messiah was coming. John was a distant cousin of Jesus, born just six months before Him. He was a rugged man who lived in the wilderness, ate locusts and wild honey, and wore clothes made out of camel hair.

John boldly challenged the Jews, "Don't just say you love God—prove it with your life. Turn from your sins and turn to God!"

He became known as John the Baptizer as he dunked those who had confessed their sins in the Jordan River. Baptism was a symbol of being washed clean from your sins and choosing a new way of living.

leaders asked John if he was the Messiah, he respond-
someone is coming soon who is far greater than me. I'm
worthy to untie His sandals or even to be His slave. You see, I
baptize with water, but He will baptize with God's Spirit!"

Soon after that Jesus came to be baptized. When John saw Him, he
said, "I'm the one who needs to be baptized by you."

Jesus insisted, so John baptized Him in front of the crowds. When
Jesus came out of the water, God's Spirit came down from the sky; it
looked like a dove floating down and resting on Him.

Then a voice from heaven said, "You are my son whom I love. You bring
me great joy!"

Retell the Scene

This may seem redundant, but it is very effective in helping your kids remember and own the story.

Scene 1 Dialogue

Remember this is a dialogue, not a quiz. The questions are a good start to draw out observations about the story, and the "answers" are just there to help you guide kids toward some key ideas.

1. **What do we learn about John from this scene?**

2. **What was John's message?**

3. **Why do you think people came to be baptized by John?**

4. **What do we learn about Jesus from this scene?**

SCENE 2: TEMPTATION
Tell the Story

After leaving the Jordan River, Jesus was led by God's Spirit to go into the wilderness. There Satan tempted Him for forty days and forty nights. During that entire time Jesus didn't eat anything and became very hungry.

Satan tried to deceive Jesus, saying, "Since you're God's Son, why don't you turn these rocks into loaves of bread to eat?"

Jesus answered him, "No. When God spoke to Moses, He said, 'People need more than bread to live. They must find their life in the words of God.'"

Then Satan took Jesus to the top of the tallest building in Jerusalem and said, "If you are God's Son, jump off! Your sacred writings say, 'God will send His angels to catch you, and you won't even hit the ground!'"

Jesus replied, "Moses also wrote, 'Do not even try to test God.'"

Next Satan took Jesus to the peak of a huge mountain. He showed Him all the nations of the world in their brilliance. He said, "I will give you all of this—anything you want—if you'll kneel down and worship me."

Jesus responded, "Get away from me, Satan! It's commanded, 'Put God above everything else and only worship Him!'"

Then Satan went away, and angels came and took care of Jesus. At this time he was about thirty years old. Throughout Jesus' life He never sinned or rebelled against God. He always chose to do what was good and right and true.

Retell the Scene

This may seem redundant, but it is very effective in helping your kids remember and own the story.

Scene 2 Dialogue

Remember this is a dialogue, not a quiz. The questions are a good start to draw out observations about the story, and the "answers" are just there to help you guide kids toward some key ideas.

5. **Where have we seen Satan or evil tempt a person in the stories before? How did that person respond?**

6. **How did Jesus respond in this scene to Satan's temptations?**
   - Resisted, quoted God's words to Satan.

7. **In your own words, with what three things did Satan tempt Jesus?**

SCENE 3: DISCIPLES

Tell the Story

Not long after that, John saw Jesus coming toward him and yelled out, "Look! There is God's Passover Lamb. He'll take away the sins of the world! God showed me He's the Messiah we've been waiting for."

As Jesus walked along the sea He told some of John's followers, "Come and follow me!" From then on Jesus surrounded Himself with a few close followers, called disciples, showing them how to live in the ways of God.

Then Jesus traveled throughout the area, meeting in market places, homes, and Jewish synagogues, teaching people God's ways. He brought a new message to them, saying, "The Kingdom of God has come. Turn from your sins and turn to God!"

Jesus healed people with every kind of sickness and disease. News spread quickly about Him, and huge crowds began following Him wherever He went. People traveled from miles away to be near Him and see the amazing miracles He performed.

Retell the Scene

This may seem redundant, but it is very effective in helping your kids remember and own the story.

Scene 3 Dialogue

Remember this is a dialogue, not a quiz. The questions are a good start to draw out observations about the story, and the "answers" are just there to help you guide kids toward some key ideas.

8. **Why did John say, "Look! There is God's Passover Lamb"?**

9. **What details do you remember about the first Passover lamb from our previous stories?**

10. **Why do you think John was convinced Jesus was the Messiah?**

11. **Why do you think crowds of people wanted to be near Jesus?**

12. **What was Jesus teaching about?**

13. **What do we learn about Jesus from this story (all three scenes)?**

   - He never rebelled against God.
   - He is like God.
   - God called Him His son whom He loves.
   - He has amazing powers.
   - He knows the writings of His people, the Hebrews.
   - People wanted to be near Him. He taught in new ways.

Application

Optional questions that may help apply the story

- **What questions do you have about the story? What do you wonder about?**

- **What will you remember most about this story?**

- **How does this story make a difference in your life?**

- **How do you think you would have responded to Jesus?**

- **What does it mean to be tempted? What can we be tempted by?**

- **Which one of the three temptations would be the toughest for you to resist right now? Why?**

- **Describe the "perfect life." How do we live the best possible way of life? What does that look like?**

Scripture Memory Verses

And a voice from heaven said, "This is my Son, whom I love; with him I am well pleased."

MATTHEW 1:17

"The time has come," he said. "The kingdom of God is near. Repent and believe the good news!"

MARK 1:15

Review the last stories a bit, focusing more on the most recent story, "Baptism and Temptation."

- What patterns do you notice about God in these stories?

- How did Jesus' birth fulfill the words of the prophets?

- Up until now, what similarities do you see between Jesus and God?

- What message did God share with everyone about Jesus when Jesus was baptized?

SCENE 1: HEALING A PARALYZED MAN

Tell the Story
Don't just read it—know it and bring it to life!

Crowds continued to surround Jesus everywhere He went. Once, when He was teaching in a house where He was staying, so many people came to hear Him that the house was completely packed. There wasn't room for one more person—even outside of the door!

Four men brought their paralyzed friend who was lying on a mat to see Jesus, believing He would heal him. The only way they could get him in the house was to climb on the roof, dig a hole through the clay tiles, and lower him down! Jesus was impressed with their effort and faith. He told the paralyzed man, "Don't worry. Your sins are forgiven!"

Some religious leaders, called Pharisees, were watching and listening to Jesus. The Pharisees were a powerful group of Jewish teachers.

They created their own set of strict rules on how to follow God in addition to the laws given to Moses.

They said to each other, "Who does this man think He is? No one can forgive sins but God!"

Jesus knew what they were thinking, so He asked them, "Why are you offended? Would you rather I would've just said, 'Pick up your mat and walk'? I will prove to you I have the authority on earth to forgive sins."

Then Jesus told the paralyzed man, "Now get up, take your mat, and walk home. You are healed."

The man was no longer paralyzed! He jumped up and pushed his way out the door and went home. Everyone there was amazed and thanked God, saying, "We've never seen anything like this before!"

Retell the Scene

This may seem redundant, but it is very effective in helping your kids remember and own the story.

Scene 1 Dialogue

Remember this is a dialogue, not a quiz. The questions are a good start to draw out observations about the story, and the "answers" are just there to help you guide kids toward some key ideas.

1. **What would you think if you were in the house that day?**

2. **Why do you think Jesus said, "Don't worry. Your sins are forgiven"?**

3. **What was Jesus teaching in this story?**

SCENE 2: EATING WITH SINNERS

Tell the Story

Soon after that, Jesus was walking along the lake shore when He saw a tax collector named Matthew sitting at his collection booth. (In that day tax collectors were hated because they had a reputation for being dishonest and corrupt.)

Jesus said to him, "Come, be my disciple!" So Matthew got up, left everything, and followed Jesus.

That night Matthew invited Jesus and His disciples to be his dinner guests. He also invited some of his tax collector friends and many other people who were known to be sinners in the community. When some of the Pharisees saw Jesus eating with them, they said to His disciples, "Why does He eat with those terrible people?"

When Jesus heard this, He told them, "Healthy people don't need a doctor; sick people do. I have come to call sinners to a changed life—inside and out—not to spend my time with those who think they're already good enough."

On another night Jesus met with some of the Jewish religious leaders for dinner. They were shocked and offended when Jesus did not wash up according to Jewish customs before the meal.

Then Jesus said to them, "You Pharisees are so careful to clean the outside of the cup and the dish, but the inside is still filthy. Your lives are just like this: so clean when people are watching, but inside you are full of hate, greed, and pride. You're worse than your Hebrew ancestors; you have great knowledge about the things of God, but you don't enter God's kingdom. In fact, you keep people from entering it!"

Retell the Scene

This may seem redundant, but it is very effective in helping your kids remember and own the story.

Scene 2 Dialogue

Remember this is a dialogue, not a quiz. The questions are a good start to draw out observations about the story, and the "answers" are just there to help you guide kids toward some key ideas.

4. **Why do think people just dropped everything to follow Jesus?**

5. **Whom did Jesus spend time with?**

6. **Why did the religious leaders have a problem with this?**
    - They understood God in terms of boundaries: laws, food, and rituals. They added their own interpretation and strictness to this.

7. **What do we learn about Jesus from this scene?**

SCENE 3: HEALING ON THE SABBATH

Tell the Story

Jesus continued to travel around teaching and healing, sometimes on the Sabbath (the day of rest). The Jewish leaders were upset about this and confronted Jesus for breaking the Sabbath rules.

Jesus replied, "God, my Father, never stops doing good, so why should I?"

This really angered them. Not only was He breaking their Sabbath rules, but He was calling God "His" Father instead of "our" father, making Himself equal with God! The Jewish leaders continued to challenge Jesus with many hostile questions, trying to trap Him into saying something they could use against Him.

Jesus went on to explain to them, "I don't do any of this on my own. I only do what my Father tells me to do. He is the source of all life and has given me the power to heal, raise the dead, and give life. Those who listen and believe in me will find new life with God that is never ending."

As Jesus finished speaking, the Pharisees and religious leaders were furious. From that time on the Jewish leaders began planning out how they could have Jesus killed.

Retell the Scene

This may seem redundant, but it is very effective in helping your kids remember and own the story.

Scene 3 Dialogue

Remember this is a dialogue, not a quiz. The questions are a good start to draw out observations about the story, and the "answers" are just there to help you guide kids toward some key ideas.

8. **What is the Sabbath?**

9. **What was Jesus' message about Himself from this last scene?**

10. **Where does Jesus' authority and power come from?**

11. What do we learn about Jesus' relationship with God from this story?

12. Who else had a perfect relationship with God from the previous stories?

13. What was that relationship like?

Dialogue

From all three of the scenes we just looked at . . .

14. What do we know about the Pharisees?

15. What are we learning about Jesus?

16. What do you think was Jesus' mission, His purpose for being?

17. What do you think it would take for this mission to happen on earth?

Application

Optional questions that may help apply the story

- What questions do you have about the story? What do you wonder about?

- What will you remember most about this story?

- How does this story make a difference in your life?

- **What do you think is more important: forgiveness or healing?**

- **How are we just like the Pharisees? How can we change this?**

- **How can we become clean on the inside?**

Scripture Memory Verses

… the Son of Man has authority on earth to forgive sins…
LUKE 5:24

I have not come to call the righteous, but sinners to repentance.
LUKE 5:32

I tell you the truth, whoever hears my word and believes him who sent me has eternal life and will not be condemned; he has crossed over from death to life.
JOHN 5:24

The Kingdom

Story from Matthew 5, 7, 10, 13, 10–20, Mark 3–5, 10, 13, Luke 6, 8–10, 12–15, 17, and John 3

Review the last stories a bit, focusing more on the most recent story, "Jesus and the Pharisees."

- What patterns do you notice about God in these stories?

- Up until now, what similarities do you see between Jesus and God?

- What message did God share with everyone about Jesus when Jesus was baptized?

- What seemed to be Jesus' main message to the Pharisees?

SCENE 1: KINGDOM MESSAGE

Tell the Story
Don't just read it—know it and bring it to life!

Jesus continued to teach people, "The Kingdom of God has come. Turn from your sins, and turn to God!"

One day He climbed up a hill with a group of His closest followers. They sat down together, and Jesus began to teach them about God's Kingdom.

He said, "God blesses those who realize their need for Him: the humble and poor, the gentle and merciful—the Kingdom of God belongs to them. God blesses the pure in heart and those who hunger and thirst to be with Him. You'll be blessed when you are hated, mocked, and excluded because you are my followers. Be happy about it—you will get great rewards in heaven!"

Then Jesus went on to teach about God's laws that were given to Moses. Jesus said, "Don't think I came to get rid of the laws of Moses and the writings of the Prophets. I have come to fulfill them! God's laws are alive and will last forever. Live by them and show others the way. That's how you'll find honor in the Kingdom."

Then He went on to teach, "The laws and commands tell you not to murder, but I say if you hate someone or insult them, you are just as guilty as a murderer. Your words and actions bring judgment on you. The laws also tell us never to have sex with someone else's spouse. But I say anyone who even looks at a woman lustfully has already committed adultery in his heart."

He also taught them, "If someone steals your shirt from you, offer them your coat too. Live generously! Love your enemies. Anyone can love their friends, but you are to love the unlovable. You must live differently, doing what is good, right, and perfect—just like God your Father."

The people were amazed at Jesus' teaching; He had real power and authority, unlike their teachers of the law.

Later the Pharisees asked Jesus, "When is this 'Kingdom' you are teaching about going to come?"

Jesus replied, "The Kingdom of God is not something you can predict. People will not say, 'Here it is,' or, 'There it is,' because the Kingdom of God is within you."

Retell the Scene

This may seem redundant, but it is very effective in helping your kids remember and own the story.

Scene 1 Dialogue

Remember this is a dialogue, not a quiz. The questions are a good start to draw out observations about the story, and the "answers" are just there to help you guide kids toward some key ideas.

1. **What do we learn about the Kingdom of God from this scene?**

2. **What does the Kingdom look like? Where is it?**

3. **In your own words, what is Jesus teaching His followers in this scene?**
    - The Pharisees had created a way for humans to be accepted by God by their actions.
    - Jesus took the commands and laws God gave Moses and revealed the inner attitudes behind the actions, showing outward actions are not enough. To God, our heart is more important than our actions.

4. **In this story, Jesus shows people how to live in God's ways. Where in the other stories have we seen God do the same thing?**
    - Adam and Eve—God walked with them teaching them how to live closely to Him.
    - Cain—"If you do what is right."
    - Noah—"Life is in the blood."
    - Moses—Laws and commands.
    - Prophets—God spoke through them to remind people of how to live in His ways.

5. **How are Jesus' Kingdom teachings similar to what God taught them in the past stories?**
    - Since the beginning of creation God has been showing people

how to live closely with Him and live in His ways—the ways of His Kingdom. Jesus continues to show us how to live in these ways through His teaching and through living out the Kingdom perfectly with His life.

6. **What do you think Jesus meant by saying, "I have come to fulfill the laws of Moses and the writings of the prophets"?**

7. **What do we learn about Jesus from this scene?**

SCENE 2: PARABLES OF THE KINGDOM
Tell the Story

Jesus continued to teach about the Kingdom of God using short stories that had powerful meanings, called parables.

He said, "The Kingdom of God is like a tiny seed that is planted in a field. This seed may be small at first, but it grows into a large tree where birds can come and find shelter."

Jesus told dozens of stories like this to the crowds.

He said the Kingdom is …

- … Like a hidden treasure buried in a field—worth diligently searching for.
- … Like yeast spread in a large ball of dough—just a little will change a lot.
- … Like a precious pearl—worth trading everything for.
- … Like a great feast—where the poor and the outcast all get invited, and on and on …

People were amazed at Jesus' teaching and wisdom. They understood some of these pictures, but others remained a mystery to them.

A young man came up to Jesus and asked, "What good things must I do to get into the Kingdom?"

Jesus replied, "God is the only one who is good. Follow His commandments."

The man said, "I have obeyed His commands. What else must I do?"

"Go and sell everything you have and give the money to the poor. Then come and follow me."

When the man heard this he went away very sad because he didn't want give up his great wealth and the things he owned.

Then Jesus told His disciples, "It's very hard for a rich person to enter the Kingdom of God. It's easier for a camel to fit through the eye of a needle!"

"Then who in the world can enter the Kingdom?" asked His disciples.

Jesus replied, "If you try on your own, you won't make it, but if you rely on God, everything is possible! The entrance to the Kingdom of God is narrow; only a few will find it. But the road that leads to destruction is very wide, many will choose this way and live only for themselves."

After spending an entire night in prayer, Jesus chose twelve men out of all of His followers to be His apprentices, calling them apostles. They traveled with Jesus wherever He went as He taught them to live in the ways of God. He sent the apostles out to heal the sick, teach others what they had learned, and share the message of the Kingdom of God.

Retell the Scene

This may seem redundant, but it is very effective in helping your kids remember and own the story.

Scene 2 Dialogue

Remember this is a dialogue, not a quiz. The questions are a good start to draw out observations about the story, and the "answers" are just there to help you guide kids toward some key ideas.

8. **Why do you think Jesus taught in parables?**

9. **What do you think the Kingdom of God is? Why is it hard to describe?**

10. **What kind of king/kingdom do you think the Jewish people were hoping for?**

11. **What did they want to conquer (win)?**

12. **What kind of kingdom was Jesus setting up?**

13. **What do you think He was looking to conquer?**

14. **Why do you think Jesus chose twelve to be His apostles? What did He send them to do?**

SCENE 3: JESUS & NICODEMUS

Tell the Story

One night a Pharisee named Nicodemus came to Jesus and said, "Rabbi, we know you were sent by God to teach us. Your miracles have proven to us that God is with you."

Jesus replied, "You're right, but unless someone is born a second time they will never understand God's Kingdom."

"What do you mean?" Nicodemus questioned, "How can someone who is fully grown climb back inside their mother and be born a second time?"

Jesus answered Him, "The truth is, no one can enter the Kingdom of God unless they have been born a second time by God's Spirit. Humans can only give human life, but God's Spirit gives new life in the Kingdom."

"How can this happen!?" Nicodemus asked.

Jesus replied, "You are a respected Jewish teacher, but you don't know this simple truth? If you won't believe me when I teach you about everyday things, how will you believe me when I tell you about God's Kingdom?

"What I am telling you is true. God showed His great love for people by sending me—His only Son—to this world. Anyone who believes in me and lives in my ways will find life that is complete and eternal! He sent me here to save people, not to judge them. Those who want to live in sin and darkness will reject me and bring God's judgment on themselves. But those who want to live in God's ways will trust me and live forever!"

Retell the Scene

This may seem redundant, but it is very effective in helping your kids remember and own the story.

Scene 3 Dialogue

Remember this is a dialogue, not a quiz. The questions are a good start to draw out observations about the story, and the "answers" are just there to help you guide kids toward some key ideas.

15. **Why do you think what Jesus was teaching was hard for Nicodemus (or anyone) to understand?**

16. **How does someone "enter the Kingdom" according to this scene? According to all three scenes?**

17. **What do we learn about Jesus from this story?**

18. **What do you think is the connection between living in God's ways and believing in Jesus?**

Application

Optional questions that may help apply the story

- **What do you like best about the story, and why?**

- **What questions do you have about the story?**

Scripture Memory Verses

And He said: "I tell you the truth, unless you change and become like little children, you will never enter the kingdom of heaven."
MATTHEW 18:3

Instead, whoever wants to become great among you must be your servant.
MATTHEW 20:26

But love your enemies, do good to them, and lend to them without expecting to get anything back. Then your reward will be great, and you will be sons of the Most High, because he is kind to the ungrateful and wicked. Be merciful, just as your Father is merciful.
LUKE 6:35-36

For God so loved the world that he gave his one and only Son, that whoever believes in him shall not perish but have eternal life.
JOHN 3:16

The Miracles

Story from Matthew 8 and Mark 4-5

Review the last stories a bit, focusing more on the most recent story, "The Kingdom."

- What patterns do you notice about God in these stories?

- Up until now, what similarities do you see between Jesus and God?

- What seemed to be Jesus' main message to the Pharisees?

- Describe the kind of Kingdom Jesus talked about.

SCENE 1: CALMING THE STORM

Tell the Story
Don't just read it—know it and bring it to life!

Evening came, and Jesus was exhausted from teaching all day. He asked His disciples to get into a boat so they could cross the lake and get away from the crowds. As they took off, Jesus went to the back of the boat, put His head on a cushion, and fell asleep. All of sudden, a terrible storm came up with strong winds and crashing waves. No matter how hard the disciples tried, they couldn't keep the boat from filling with water.

The disciples ran to the back of the boat in a panic to wake Jesus, shouting, "Teacher, don't you care that we're going to drown?"

Jesus awoke, stood up, and said to the wind and waves, "Quiet! Be still." As soon as He said this the wind stopped blowing and the sea became calm. Then Jesus asked them, "Why are you so afraid? Don't you believe in me yet?"

The disciples just sat there amazed. They asked each other, "Who is this? Even the wind and the waves obey Him!"

Retell the Scene

This may seem redundant, but it is very effective in helping your kids remember and own the story.

Scene 1 Dialogue

Remember this is a dialogue, not a quiz. The questions are a good start to draw out observations about the story, and the "answers" are just there to help you guide kids toward some key ideas.

1. **Which of our other stories talk about the wind and the waves? What happened in those stories?**

   - When Israel crossed the Red Sea and God brought a strong east wind to open the sea and returned it by bringing a strong west wind to kill the army of Pharaoh.

   - Noah and the ark.

2. **If you were in the boat, what would you have said or done after Jesus calmed the winds and waves?**

3. **What do we learn about the disciples from this scene?**

4. **Why do you think they woke Jesus up? Why do you think they waited so long?**

5. **Why do you think Jesus waited to calm the storm until the boat was full of water? Maybe He was just a really hard sleeper!**

6. **What do we learn about Jesus from this scene?**

_____

SCENE 2: RECOGNIZED BY DEMONS

Tell the Story

When Jesus reached the other side of the lake, a wild man filled with demons ran toward Him from a nearby cemetery. This man had been chained to some of the tombs to keep him from hurting people, but he snapped the chains from his wrists and ankles. Now he wandered around all day and night, screaming and hitting himself with stones. No one could control him because he was too strong!

As he approached, Jesus said to him, "Come out of this man, you demons!"

The man fell down in front of Jesus and screamed, "Why are you bothering me, Jesus, Son of God? Please don't torture me!"

Then Jesus asked, "What is your name?"

"Legion," the man replied, "because there are many of us inside of this man."

Over and over the demons begged Jesus not to send them far away. There happened to be a heard of pigs feeding on a hillside nearby. "Send us into those pigs!" the demons pleaded.

Jesus replied, "All right, go!" The demons came out of the man and entered the pigs. The entire heard of 2,000 pigs immediately rushed down the steep hillside into the lake where they drowned!

Those who witnessed what had happened ran into town to tell everyone they could find. Soon the entire town came out to see what had happened. They were astonished when they saw the man fully clothed and no longer insane! Then the crowd begged Jesus to go away and leave them alone.

Jesus and His followers went back to their boat. As they were leaving, the man who had been filled with demons asked if he could go with them.

Jesus said to him, "You need to go back to your friends and tell them the great things the Lord has done for you and how He showed you mercy."

The man went and visited towns all over that region, telling people about the great things Jesus had done. Everyone he talked to was amazed by what had happened.

Retell the Scene

This may seem redundant, but it is very effective in helping your kids remember and own the story.

Scene 2 Dialogue

Remember this is a dialogue, not a quiz. The questions are a good start to draw out observations about the story, and the "answers" are just there to help you guide kids toward some key ideas.

7. **What do we find out about the man who met up with Jesus in this scene? (Describe everything that comes to mind.)**

8. **What are demons? Where did they come from?**
   - Fallen angels, created by God.

9. **How did God treat the demons in our first story?**

    ▪ God judged them and cast them out of His presence.

10. **How do you think the demons knew who Jesus was? Why were they afraid of Him?**

11. **How did people who saw what happened respond? What did they do and say?**

12. **Why do you think the crowd begged Jesus to go away?**

13. **How did the man who was set free from the demons respond?**

14. **Why did Jesus tell him he couldn't go on the boat?**

15. **What do we learn about Jesus from this scene?**

SCENE 3: POWER OVER DEATH

Tell the Story

When Jesus and His disciples went back across the lake, a large crowd was already waiting for Him on the beach.

One of the local Jewish leaders named Jairus ran to Jesus and fell down at His feet. He begged Jesus to heal his twelve-year-old daughter. "My little girl is very sick and about to die," he cried. "Please come and heal her so she can live."

Jesus went with Jairus toward his house, and the crowd followed behind them. Along the way some of Jairus' friends stopped him, saying, "We just came from your house. Your daughter has died. There's no use bringing the Teacher to your house now."

Jesus ignored them and said to Jairus, "Don't be afraid. Just trust me." Then Jesus told the crowd to stay back, and He only let three of His disciples, Peter, James, and John, come with them.

When they arrived at Jairus' house there was a crowd of people inside weeping loudly. Jesus asked them, "Why are you crying? The girl is not dead—she's sleeping."

The crowd laughed at Him. Then Jesus sent everyone outside except for the girl's parents and the disciples who were with Him. When they went into the girl's room, Jesus took the girl's hand and said, "Little girl, get up!"

Immediately the girl jumped out of bed and began walking around! Her parents were absolutely amazed! Jesus told them to give her something to eat and asked them not to tell anyone about what they'd just seen.

Retell the Scene

This may seem redundant, but it is very effective in helping your kids remember and own the story.

Scene 3 Dialogue

Remember this is a dialogue, not a quiz. The questions are a good start to draw out observations about the story, and the "answers" are just there to help you guide kids toward some key ideas.

16. How do you think the girl's parents were feeling during this scene?

17. Why do you think people didn't believe Jesus in this scene?

18. Why do you think Jesus sometimes asked people not to say anything about His miracles?

19. How did people usually respond to Jesus' miracles?

20. What do we learn about Jesus from this scene?

From all three of the scenes we just looked at . . .

21. What are some of the reasons Jesus performed miracles?

22. Did people always believe in Jesus after seeing Him perform miracles? Why or why not?

23. From the stories, what has Jesus shown He has power over? Where have we seen power like this in the stories before?

24. Is anything or anyone more powerful than Jesus?

25. What are we learning about Jesus from our stories so far?

Application
Optional questions that may help apply the story

- **What questions do you have about the story? What do you wonder about?**

- **What will you remember most about this story?**

- **How does this story make a difference in your life?**

- **What do you see for the first time in this story?**

- **What amazes you the most about Jesus?**

- **What miracle do you think would have amazed you the most?**

- **How should we respond to Jesus today?**

Scripture Memory Verses

Do not fear, only believe.
from MARK 5:36

Now faith is the assurance of things hoped for, the conviction of things not seen.
HEBREWS 11:1

Death & Resurrection

20

Story from Matthew 26–28, Mark 14–16, Luke 22–24, John 13, and 17–20

Review the last stories a bit, focusing more on the most recent story, "Miracles."

- What patterns do you notice about God in these stories?

- Describe the kind of kingdom Jesus talked about.

- Which miracle that we learned about really sticks with you?

You may want to talk about the meaning of the following words especially with younger children: arrest, riot, covenant, abandon, betray, plead, mob, execute, and mock. This is not light reading!

Tell the Story
Don't just read it—know it and bring it to life!

Jesus and His disciples traveled to Jerusalem for the Passover Festival. The Pharisees and other Jewish leaders were becoming more and more upset with Jesus and His teachings. They looked for ways to trap Jesus into saying something so they could arrest Him, but Jesus was too wise for them. Many of His stories pointed out the hypocrisy of the Jewish leaders—how they taught about doing things one way and then actually did them another or without the right love in their heart for God.

Jesus said, "When the Pharisees and teachers share with you God's commands, listen to them—but don't follow their example. They don't live out what they teach."

The high priest met with these leaders to discuss capturing Jesus and putting Him to death. "We can't arrest Him during Passover," they agreed, "or it will create a huge riot."

Jesus and His twelve disciples met together in a home to celebrate the Passover. During the meal Jesus picked up some bread, thanked God for it, and broke it into pieces. Giving it to His disciples He said, "Take this and eat it; this is my body given for you."

Then Jesus picked up a cup of wine and thanked God for it. He gave them the cup and said, "All of you, drink this. It is my blood given for you—a new covenant between God and His people. It is poured out to forgive the sins of many. Remember me when you continue to eat and drink these things together."

Jesus told them, "When you see what happens tonight, you will all abandon me. It is part of God's plan that I will be betrayed and die. But don't fear, I will rise again from the dead!" He knew His disciple Judas would betray Him, bringing Jewish soldiers to capture Him later that night when no one was around.

After the meal when it was dark, Jesus went to pray. Filled with pain and sorrow, He pleaded with God, "Father, if there is another way besides my death, please let that happen—but I will do whatever you ask."

Just as He had finished praying, Judas showed up with an armed mob. He greeted Jesus with a kiss, a sign to show the guards which one they should arrest.

Jesus said to them, "Am I a dangerous criminal that you need weapons to capture me? Why didn't you arrest me in the Temple where I've been teaching every day? No! This is part of God's plan, just as the prophets predicted long ago."

When the guards arrested Jesus and dragged Him away, the disciples ran away and hid. The guards beat Jesus and brought Him before the Jewish leaders for questioning.

They asked, "Are you the Messiah, the Son of God?"

Jesus answered, "I am, and you will see me seated next to God in power, coming back on the clouds of heaven."

When Jesus said this, the high priest tore his clothing in horror and said, "Any man who claims to be God must be put to death." Then they slapped Jesus in the face and spit on Him.

Since Jews could not execute anyone without official approval, Jesus was brought to the Roman governor, Pilate. The Jewish leaders stirred up the crowds and pressured Pilate to have Jesus put to death. They shouted, "Crucify Him! Crucify Him!"

Pilate feared a riot would break out, so he handed Jesus over to the Roman soldiers to be crucified. Crucifixion was the cruelest and most humiliating way to die.

Jesus was brutally beaten and whipped by the soldiers. They put a crown of sharp thorns on His head and a purple robe around His shoulders. "Hail the King of the Jews!" they laughed. All night the Roman soldiers continued to beat Jesus and mock Him.

When morning came, they led Jesus to a place called Skull Hill. Like a criminal, Jesus was nailed to a heavy wooden cross between two thieves.

Hanging there, He cried out, "Father, please forgive them. They don't know what they're doing."

At noon, darkness filled the skies blocking out the sun for three hours. Suddenly, the thick curtain hanging in the Temple tore down the middle!

At that moment Jesus shouted, "Father! I give you my life. It is finished." Then Jesus breathed His last breath and died.

The soldiers broke the legs of the criminals crucified next to Jesus to speed up their death. When they found Jesus was already dead, they didn't break His legs. To be sure, one of the soldiers stabbed Him in the side with a spear—blood and water poured out.

Late Friday afternoon Jesus' body was taken down from the cross, wrapped in long strips of cloth, and buried in a rich man's tomb. A large stone was rolled over the entrance to the tomb, and Roman guards were posted to make sure nothing happened to His body.

(Pause here for a moment.)

Early on Sunday morning, some of the women who followed Jesus went to prepare His body for burial. When they arrived at the tomb, they saw the stone rolled away and the soldiers gone!

Suddenly, two angels appeared. They said, "Why are you surprised? You are looking for Jesus, but He is not here. He's been raised from the dead." The women were excited but afraid and hurried to tell the disciples the amazing news. Some of them ran back to the tomb and looked inside for themselves. . . .

Jesus was not there!

Retell the Story

This may seem redundant, but it is very effective in helping your kids remember and own the story. You will want to help them retell the story by giving them leading questions.

Dialogue

Remember this is a dialogue, not a quiz. The questions are a good start to draw out observations about the story, and the "answers" are just there to help you guide kids toward some key ideas.

1. **Why was Jesus going to Jerusalem? What do we know about this celebration?**

2. **Do you think Jesus had a choice in how He died?**

3. **How does the Passover story we heard earlier remind you of Jesus' death?**

4. **Why did the Jewish leaders want to kill Jesus?**

5. **What did Jesus mean when He said, "Take this and eat it; this is my body given for you," and, ". . . drink this. It is my blood given for you—a new covenant between God and His people"?**

6. **What was God's covenant with His people? What do you think the "new covenant" is?**

7. **Why do you think the curtain in the Temple tore in half? What did the curtain separate?**

8. **How did Jesus fulfill the prophet's predictions about the coming Messiah?**
   - He will be beaten, whipped, and wounded.
   - He will be put on trial and thrown in prison.
   - His hands and feet would be pierced.
   - He will be killed like a criminal, then buried in a rich man's tomb.
   - God will lay the punishment and guilt for all of our sins on Him.

- His life will be made an offering for us.
- Because of Him, many will be made right with God.

9. How is Jesus being raised from the dead significant? What does it show us about Him?

Application
Optional questions that may help apply the story

- **What questions do you have about the story? What do you wonder about?**

- **What will you remember most about this story?**

- **How does this story make a difference in your life?**

- **What do you see for the first time in this story?**

- **What amazes you the most about Jesus?**

- **How was Jesus' death part of God's plan?**

Scripture Memory Verses

The Son of Man must be delivered into the hands of sinful men, be crucified and on the third day be raised again.

LUKE 24:7

Jesus knew that the time had come for him to leave this world and go to the Father. Having loved his own who were in the world, he now showed them the full extent of his love.

JOHN 13:1

The Church

21

Story from Matthew 28, John 14, 20, Acts 1–2, and
1 Corinthians 15

*Since this is the last narrative, make sure to leave time to review and discuss the
entire Story of God as a whole and its implications for how we should live today.
We're part of the Story, too, after all.*

Tell the Story

Don't just read it—know it and bring it to life!

In the weeks that followed Jesus' death, He appeared to His disciples
many times and was seen by more than 500 eyewitnesses. Quickly
the news about His resurrection spread throughout the land.

One of Jesus' disciples named Thomas said, "I won't believe He is
alive unless I can put my fingers into the holes where His hands where
nailed to the cross."

A few days later, Jesus appeared to His disciples and said to Thomas,
"Put your fingers here—feel the hole in my hand. Put your hand into
the wound on my side."

Thomas shouted, "It is you, Jesus—my God!"

Then Jesus said, "I will bless those even more who haven't seen but
still believe!"

Soon after that, Jesus met with His disciples over a meal. He said,
"John baptized you in water, but in a few days you will be baptized with

God's Spirit. This will give you power to live in my ways and tell the entire world about me."

Jesus commanded them, "Go! Make disciples all over the world. Teach them to walk in my ways and obey me. I am leaving now to be with my Father in Heaven, but you will never be alone. God's Spirit will come and live inside of you, giving you peace and leading you in all the ways of truth."

As the disciples watched, Jesus went up into the sky, disappearing in the clouds right in front of them!

(Pause)

A few weeks later, a group of 120 of Jesus' followers gathered to pray together in Jerusalem. All of a sudden, they heard a loud sound—like a roaring windstorm—that filled the house where they were meeting. Each of them was filled with God's Spirit and started speaking in languages not their own! They went out into the street and began to tell people about the great things that Jesus had done.

At that time, Jews from all over the world were living in Jerusalem. This roaring sound was heard throughout the entire city, and a large crowd had gathered outside the house to see what was going on. When the people heard Jesus' followers speaking, they said, "How can this be? They're from Galilee, but they're speaking in our own languages. This is amazing!"

One of Jesus' disciples, named Peter, stepped forward to explain to the crowds what was happening. He said, "This is part of God's prophecy being fulfilled. We are eyewitnesses of the fact that Jesus was raised from the dead and is the true Messiah!"

Then Peter explained how Jesus had fulfilled everything the prophets said about the Messiah. He told the crowd, "Each of you must turn from your sins and turn to God. In Jesus, you will find forgiveness. He is the final sacrifice everyone's sin. This is God's new covenant offered not just to the Jews, but for all who want to be part of God's family." That day thousands believed what Peter had said and turned from their sins to follow Jesus. They were baptized and became a part of God's family, once again empowered to live out God's promise to be a blessing to all people.

God's new covenant was not written on tablets of stone like before, but on the hearts and minds of His people, so they would always know how to live in His ways. These followers of Jesus were deeply committed to God and each other, sharing everything they had, praying, learning God's ways together, and helping anyone in need—all with great joy and generosity. Daily they ate together to honor and remember Jesus' life given for them. They saw God do amazing things through them—miracles and healing—as He added people to their group each day.

This was the beginning of what the Bible calls the Church, a community of people all over the world who, because of Jesus, once again enjoy a life that is full and complete, following in the ways of God. We can join this amazing story; the story can continue with us!

Retell the Story

This may seem redundant, but it is very effective in helping your kids remember and own the story. You will want to help them retell the story by giving them leading questions.

Dialogue

Remember this is a dialogue, not a quiz. The questions are a good start to draw out observations about the story, and the "answers" are just there to help you guide kids toward some key ideas.

1. **Do you think Jesus was really raised from the dead?**

2. **What do you hear in this story that makes you believe Jesus rose from the dead?**

3. **What was Jesus' command right before leaving His disciples? Is this command also for us today?**

4. **What is a disciple?**

5. **How do you make a disciple?**

6. **What did Jesus say about God's Spirit?**
   - God's Spirit will come and live inside of you, giving you peace and leading you in all the ways of truth.

7. **What was the covenant God made with Abraham and His people? What did it require?**

8. **How did God make a new covenant with His people? What is the new covenant?**

Review All the Stories

ALLOW EXTRA TIME FOR THIS! Come up with a creative way for the group to give a brief overview of all the stories.

Dialogue

Think about all of the stories that we have heard together. . . .

9. What have you learned from these stories? What amazes you?

10. What common themes run through all of the stories?

- God wants us to live closely with Him, listening and obeying.

- He provides the best possible way of life for us to live.

- God desires to rescue His creation and bring them back to Himself.

- He will go to amazing lengths to accomplish this.

- Our sins require sacrifice—a life for a life.

11. How do all of these stories connect as one big story?

12. If you had to tell the entire story—the whole story—what would you tell us?

13. What have we learned about what God is like? Where have we seen that?

(Make a list of these things)

- He does what is good, right, and perfect. He is holy.

- He is powerful, is creative, knows all things, has control over the elements, punishes rebellion, keeps His promises, does not allow evil to remain with Him, provides a way of forgiveness, loves His creation, provides us with the best way to live, wants to protect us and bless us, wants us to continue His blessings, and much more!

14. How does this story continue (with us)?

Application

Optional questions that may help apply the story

- **What questions do you have about the story? What do you wonder about?**

- **What will you remember most about the story?**

- **How does this story make a difference in your life?**

- **Where does your story fit into this entire Story of God?**

- **If you were to draw a symbol (an icon) for your life story, what would it look like?**

- **What does it mean for you to live in God's ways right now?**

Scripture Memory Verses

Then Jesus came to them and said, "All authority in heaven and on earth has been given to me. Therefore go and make disciples of all nations, baptizing them in the name of the Father and of the Son and of the Holy Spirit, and teaching them to obey everything I have commanded you. And surely I am with you always, to the very end of the age."

MATTHEW 28:18-20

Peace be with you! As the Father has sent me, I am sending you.

JOHN 20:21

But you will receive power when the Holy Spirit comes on you; and you will be my witnesses in Jerusalem, and in all Judea and Samaria, and to the ends of the earth.

ACTS 1:8

CHILDREN IN MISSIONAL COMMUNITIES

Our Simple Structure For Weekly Meals

We treat our children as full participants in our communities. They serve, they eat, and they grow in their understanding of the gospel right alongside us. However, it is also beneficial to create intentional spaces for them to learn the gospel and to have freedom to play and enjoy their friends. This is our simple process to care for kids in weekly missional community discussion times. We generally have our younger children share in the eating and the mealtime, but then separate kids and adults for our 45 minutes of prayer and discussion.

Give Someone the Responsibility

If your missional community has young kids, you will want to have someone oversee their participation. Specifically, you want to give this servant responsibility to someone who can organize the group to care for kiddos during the weekly discussions. He or she is the person who reminds your community who is helping with kids and why.

Everyone Participates

We want our communities to share the load of investing in our children's growth and discipleship. Communities make a calendar and have everyone sign up for a meeting. We give them simple tracks to run on that make the time significant. Perhaps the most significant impact an adult can have in these times is creates space for relationship and share who they are with the kids.

Investing in Kids with Intentional Environment

Here is the simplest and most effective structure for the kid's time. We've seen this greatly impact the full life of communities as adults grow in knowing the gospel and in their ability to share life with others beyond children. It's a great teaching process. Furthermore, it is incredibly easy to maintain and free.

Have the adult teach the kids how to do something they are talented at or interested in (such as music, soccer, painting, cooking, jumping rope, crochet, etc.). It could be anything as long as it is a genuine sharing of something they are interested in.

Then have the adult share an important part of his or her story in learning who Jesus is and what He has done for him or her. You can even encourage him or her to share something from his or her childhood.

Lastly, the adult will share one of his or her favorite Bible verses and explain what it means and how it has impacted his or her life. Explaining what this passage tells us about God (who He is, what He has done) and about us (who we are, how we're transformed by the gospel, and how we are called to follow Him).

Cautions:

- Avoid leaning on the older kids to care for the younger kids. There are safety issues involved for the younger children. For the older kids, they are at an age where they should be processing and learning alongside the adults and shouldn't be regulated to childcare.

- Keep the doors open to the children's spaces and have multiple adults helping.

- Background check all people helping with kids.

- Avoid the temptation to let Netflix watch your community's kids.

Let's Color!

Enhance the understanding of each story with the *Story of God for Kids* downloadable coloring pages!

The *Story of God for Kids* coloring pages are uniquely designed to allow children of all ages to:

- creatively explore each week's story and themes

- further engage their place in God's story

- artistically express their understanding of Scripture (great for visual and spatial learners!)

Grab the coloring pages here:

SaturateTheWorld.com/Resources/Story-God-For-Kids/Coloring-Sheets